TEACHING *Adults* WITH CONFIDENCE

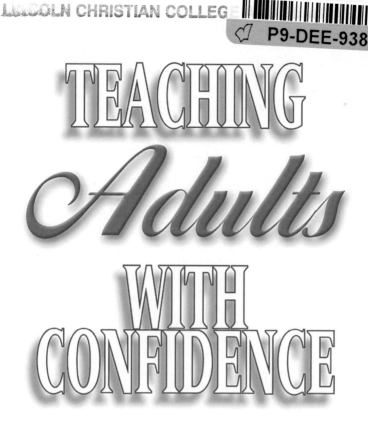

by
Dr. Paul J. Loth
& Jennifer Jezek

Evangelical Training Association

1620 Penny Lane

Schaumburg, IL 60173

Cover Design: Kurtz Design Studio, Tulsa, OK

Scripture quotations, are from the New American Standard Bible, © The Lockman Foundation 1960, 1962, 1963, 1971, 1972, 1973, 1975, 1977. Used by permission.

2004 Edition

ISBN: 1-929852-03-7

Contents

110919

Preface

The most significant challenge in getting this book to press has been the prominent role of change in our lives. When this work began, a gifted biblical teacher, Dr. Wayne Haston, was secured for his insights into biblical education for the local church. His already published work *Adult Sunday School Ministry: The Dynamics of Successful Classrooms* was to be condensed for the ETA audience, fulfilling a quest to bring the *Teaching With Confidence* series into our Classroom Series options. Condensing and updating Haston's book soon became a bigger chore than his devoted editor, Dr. Jonathan Thigpen, could accomplish. Dr. Thigpen was stricken with ALS and went to be with the Lord before his efforts on this project could be completed.

Soon economic downturns and the aftermath of terrorism took their toll on the curriculum development budget. The project was tabled until those matters were resolved. Upon resurrection, Dr. Paul J. Loth, a Christian educator with an ETA history, stepped into salvage the effort. He was greatly assisted by Ms. Jennifer Jezek, a staff writer. Both authors merged their love for the mission of ETA with contemporary perspective and exuberance for adult curriculum development to create the work in your hand. Dr. Loth represents the experience of maturity and context arrived from multiple decades of interaction with the adult learner. Ms. Jezek contributes the hope and enthusiasm of young adults who embrace diversity. Together you will experience the true joy of teaching all adults with confidence.

This journey of teaching is not daunting when viewed in its proper perspective. The sage wisdom from the *Remains of Rev. Joshua Wells Downing* (1842) still applies:

"The Bible is your textbook; you are to explain its laws, enforce its precepts, unfold its beauties, and recommend its love. Mankind and the wide world are your field of illustration. To fit you for the calling, you need a mind disciplined in the school of the prophets, a heart daily imbibing wisdom at the cross of Christ." May God so bless your calling.

Yvonne Thigpen
ETA President

The Thrill of Teaching Adults

~ 1 ~

Teaching adults is an exciting adventure! Many things contribute to making the *adult* teaching experience stand out from the teaching experience of the younger age groups. But by far the most rewarding aspect is the visible impact of teaching adults on multiple lives. In fact, there may be no better way to exponentially expand your ministry efforts than participating in adult ministry. Listen in on the conversation below between an adult teacher and her friend:

As they approached the sanctuary door, Betty couldn't help but notice the smile on Maria's face.

"You haven't stopped smiling since we left the house. What's going on?"

"Oh, I was just thinking …about my class. I enjoy it so much."

"How so?" asked Betty, curiously.

"Well, for one, everyone is so active and wants to participate," said Maria. "When I taught other classes, like children's and youth classes, I always had to focus on motivating them to learn. I had to make sure they understood that my lesson was important and they would need to know it someday. But my adults come ready to learn."

Betty wasn't convinced. "Well, I once led a teacher training class for adults," she said. "It was awful! They disagreed with me if they had a different experience or idea, and if the class activity wasn't working, they told me!"

"That's what I love about teaching them!" Maria interrupted. "Think about who's in my class."

"Yes, you have some very gifted people...people with a lot of Bible knowledge and a lot of experience."

"And they know the Bible better than I do," Maria admitted.

"Then how do you teach them?" Betty asked.

"I don't," Maria explained, "I facilitate the class. The members learn from each other and from their own personal discoveries in God's Word. And the exciting thing is I feel like by teaching them, I am impacting the whole church."

Teaching Adults: A Ministry of Multiplication

Maria is right. Teaching adults is much broader than one class or group. Teaching adults is also a ministry to:

Families – Adults are leaders in their families, whether single parent families, single adults relating to families, multi-generational families, or traditional families with a mother, a father, and one or more children. Adults are the ones who make the families work. Husbands and wives provide the key marital stability upon which families are built. Grandparents discover the rich joy of not only teaching their grandchildren but also continuing to guide their adult children. Parents experience the challenge of caring for aging parents as well as the increasing needs of their own children. As parents grow in their relationship with God, they are able to share their spiritual growth with their children, their spouses, and even their parents. Every member of the family, therefore, feels the benefits of the adult teacher's lessons.

Church Leaders – It is the adult members of the church, guided by the pastor, who lead the church community. The teacher of adults facilitates the learning and spiritual growth of these church leaders. As the leaders of the church learn God's Word and apply it to their lives, the entire church community is blessed.

The Lost – We are all called to evangelism. The real key to outreach, however, is sharing our spiritual relationship with others. As we grow in our relationship with God, we have more to share with others. Many churches provide training and educational programs in evangelism and outreach, helping adults to develop their outreach skills. Often adults are so excited about this opportunity to evangelize others that they follow God's call into full-time missions—all because of an adult teacher who helped them grow.

Church Members – The true ministry of the church takes place through the gifts of the church members. These members use gifts of mercy, exhortation, hospitality, helps and many more to serve their brothers and sisters in Christ. Often, new teachers arise out of the adult class when observation of good teaching awakens a desire for ministry.

The Workplace – The integration of the Christian faith and practice into a secular, sometimes evil, work environment is a struggle for many believers. This can only take place as adults are continually fed with God's Word and are able to grow in ways that integrate the Word with everyday life. The teacher of adults has a wonderful opportunity to guide this process, facilitating the adult believer's learning of the Bible and application of the Word to the work environment.

Biblical Basis for Teaching Adults

Perhaps Paul captures the essence of adulthood: "When I was a child, I used to speak like a child, think like a child, reason like a child; when I became a man, I did away with childish things" (1 Cor. 13:11). Adults are in a season of putting simple ways aside and becoming mature in all aspects of life. They continue to develop mentally, socially, physically, morally, and spiritually throughout their lives. The Bible gives no indication that learning or growth stops at a certain age; rather, Christian adults are to be lifelong learners who, like Jesus, keep "increasing in wisdom and stature, and in favor with God and men" (Luke 2:52).

There are many biblical reasons for teaching adults. The first and most obvious reason is the commandment of Christ: "Go therefore and make disciples...*teaching* them to observe all that I commanded you." (Matt. 28:19-20, italics added). There are also several scriptural needs of adults that a teaching ministry can meet.

Spiritual Growth – First, adults are in need of a personal encounter with Jesus Christ, where they recognize their utter sinfulness and trust Him for salvation. After this, adults must grow in their faith and be continually transformed into the likeness of Christ in mind, heart, and lifestyle (2 Cor. 3:18; Rom. 12:1-2; Col. 1:28). They must move from an immature or infantile faith to one that is able to handle solid spiritual food. They must learn to walk in a godly manner and to stand strong in the face of deceptive doctrines (Eph. 4:14-17; 1 Cor. 3:1-3). Adult teachers must encourage adults to take ownership of their faith and grow up in their salvation.

Biblical Literacy – Every adult believer should be a student of the Word. All adults need to know the basic contents of the Bible, the organization of Bible books, who wrote them, and the fundamental teachings of Scripture. Biblical literacy is a crucial need in the church today, as well as the skill to study the Bible on one's own. Adults must increasingly be able to feed themselves from the Word of God rather than being overly dependent on others to combat non-biblical worldviews.

A major part of this, of course, is the application of Scripture to each adult's life, whether this is related to a person's family responsibilities, personal life, or job and career. Applying Scripture to one's life is not a separate purpose of adult learning; rather, it is an integral part of Bible literacy (James 1:22).

Strong Families – The biblical guidelines for adults on family matters are numerous (Eph. 5:22–33, 6:1–4; Col. 3:18–21; 1 Pet. 3:1–7; Titus 2:4–5). God has designed the Christian home to be a powerful witness to the watching world. His Word teaches adults to be godly mothers and fathers and loving husbands and wives. Single adults also are to be responsible family members, whether they are caring for aging or widowed parents (1 Tim. 5:4, 8), helping siblings or extended family in need, or being "mom" or "dad" to young children from families in the church. A teacher of adults can provide valuable instructions in important family roles.

Godly Character – Titus 2 lists character qualities to be developed in every stage of adulthood. Older men are to be "temperate, dignified, sensible, sound in faith, in love, in perseverance" (v. 2). Older women are to likewise be "reverent in their behavior, not malicious gossips nor enslaved to much wine, teaching what is good" (v. 3). Young women are to "love their husbands, to love their children, to be sensible, pure, workers at home, kind, being subject to their own husbands" (v. 4–5). In the same way, young men also must be self-controlled or "sensible" (v. 6). Nurturing these character traits must be a goal for every teacher of adults.

Teaching Skills – Either formally or informally, every Christian adult is in some way a teacher to others—whether children, youth, or other adults. Deuteronomy 11:18–19 commands adults to teach their children God's laws in the midst of all of their daily activities. In Paul's writings, all older women are considered teachers of the younger women (Titus 2:3–4). Mature servants of the Lord are expected to be able to gently and patiently teach and correct others (2 Tim. 2:24–25). Whether adults are mentoring, parenting, evangelizing, leading, or befriending they will influence and teach others in big or small ways. The teacher of adults can help adults to be better teachers of God's Word and ways.

Ministry Skills – Every Christian adult must be equipped for a life of service to the church. God has not only called the pastor to minister, He has called us all to minister to each other. And God has given all believers specific spiritual gifts to be used, not for our own benefit, but to help build the church and accomplish God's work in the world (Eph. 4:7–16; Rom. 12:3–8; 1 Cor. 12).

But these gifts must be developed! A major focus of the church's educational program must be helping adults within the church community determine their area of giftedness, to develop their gifts, and then to find an area of ministry. This is the heart of the "ministry of multiplication" that Maria described above.

Training Adult Leaders

Teaching adults is really about training leaders. God has uniquely created adults to be the spiritual pillars of the church. They should be examples to the younger generation through maturity in faith, extensive Bible knowledge, and godly character. Their leadership in family, ministry, and the workplace will impact lives deeply. As children, youth, and other adults listen to their words or watch their lifestyles, they learn more about a personal relationship with the Creator.

So what kind of teaching format should be used when training adult leaders? Adults enjoy making their own choices and pursuing their own goals. They are experienced and knowledgeable. Many of them have already been leaders for a length of time. They are practical. They have been around long enough to know what works and what does not. They also know themselves fairly well. They can see their own needs and problems, and they usually know where to find solutions.

The example of Jesus' teaching strategy with adults is helpful here. Jesus selected a small group of twelve men and presented them with a choice: "Follow me." These men were from different walks of life, with unique knowledge and experiences to bring to the group. The Lord's teaching was intentional, mixing direct instruction with penetrating questions and open discussion (Mt. 5; Lk. 9:18-20). In a context of loving relationships, He modeled what he taught and gave His disciples practical ministry guidance and experience (John 13:1-17; Luke 9:1-6).

Jesus' goal in calling them was so "that they would be with Him and that He could send them out" (Mk. 3:14). As adult teachers this should be our goal as well. Rather than making our adult students dependent on us, our role is to "send them out" to be leaders in their homes, in their workplaces, in the church. From studying the characteristics of adult learners to the qualities of an adult teacher, from looking at how to design a purposeful adult learning experience to choosing methods and curriculum, your ministry will be multiplied as you train adult leaders.

Summary

Teaching adults is a thrill! It is a ministry of multiplication since adults are influential in every area of life. The Bible gives many reasons for teaching adults. Christ commands us to teach adults. By so doing we help them grow spiritually, to develop biblical literacy, to be strong family members, to exhibit godly character, to be teachers of others, and to develop their ministry gifts. Teaching adults is a different kind of teaching. It requires teachers to have the mindset of Jesus who was seeking to send out leaders into effective ministry. This is the way Jesus participated in God's plan for Kingdom expansion. It should be ours as well!

For Further Discussion

1. What new insights about adult ministry have you gained from this chapter?
2. Discuss the characteristics of an adult Bible class or group where biblical literacy is not a high priority.
3. In what ways can your church realize the ministry of multiplication by teaching adults?
4. Identify the specific "sending out" results of your adult teaching ministry through mentoring, parenting, evangelizing, or leading.

How Adults Learn

~ 2 ~

Another Bible study class is over. As your adults file out of class, some are leaving quietly. Others are engaging in casual conversations with friends, discussing topics ranging from football to babies. Some are commenting on the issues addressed during the class.

Once the room has been vacated you rethink what happened. Just how do you interpret the class members' reactions to the lesson?

Your mind begins to visualize Curtis Lowery. He doesn't speak out much in class discussions, but whenever he does, Curt's thoughtful responses always reflect such a good grasp of Scripture. Everyone learns from what Curt contributes.

Lakeisha Jackson hits the class talking, leaves the same way, and never seems to stop in between. In fact, Lakeisha has often commented that she attends your class because you provide opportunities for the class members to get to know each other and to react freely to the issues being studied.

Alex Caruthers is an interesting fellow. Alex, a mechanic by trade, loves to work with his hands. Even his hobby of woodworking proves that. Alex is an easygoing guy who has never been known to have his head in the clouds. He especially likes group Bible study when he leaves with something that will help him during the week.

Sam and Sylvia Chen come from a completely different mold. Sam is a computer program designer for one of the most progressive software companies in the business. Sylvia is a part-time graphic artist. Having Sam and Sylvia in your class has been a challenge. They get the point of the lesson very quickly and then want to move on to more mind-stimulating things. They really came to life the day they volunteered, impromptu, to act out a contemporary Good Samaritan incident.

How Adults Learn Best

Each of these adult class members demonstrates a key ingredient of adult learning. Educational leaders over the last century have helped us understand better how adults learn. This started with Eduard Lindeman, a pioneer in adult education, often called the grandfather of adult education, who defined adult education as the "continual process of evaluating life's experiences."[1]

John Dewey then followed this basic philosophy in the 1940s with his emphasis on "experiential learning." Dewey not only focused upon adult learning but developed "experimental schools" to apply experiential learning to children and youth, as well.

Malcolm Knowles, a leader in adult education, is often called the father of modern-day adult education. Knowles spent time studying the differences between traditional learning and adult learning. He promoted a learner-directed approach to adult education (termed andragogy) rather than the teacher-directed approach that was often used in traditional education (termed pedagogy).[2] Knowles' approach still informs much of contemporary adult education practice, and his insights are very valuable to Christian educators. Many of the characteristics of adult learners listed in this chapter are based on this concept of andragogy.

General Characteristics of Adult Learners

To create the optimum adult learning environment, we must always remember the following points:

Adults are task-oriented – Whereas most of education up to adulthood is content-based and subject-oriented, adult learning is task-based. Look through the catalogs for your local adult educational programs. You will not find many course listings for the typical college classes or academic subjects. Instead, most of the classes will involve accomplishing a task, solving a problem, or developing a job or life-related skill. For example, you will see classes on learning a foreign language, putting a roof on a house, or sewing a patchwork quilt.

The same task-oriented focus is true in teaching adults in the church. Adults want training on faith-related tasks such as studying the Bible and witnessing to neighbors. They also want help with social and developmental tasks such as raising children, being a better spouse, or starting off in a new career. Problems encountered in daily life can also motivate adults to seek learning. For example, they may want help in managing stress, resolving coworker conflicts, or fighting a racial injustice in their community.

Adults are pragmatic – Just as Alex always wanted to leave the adult Bible study with something specific to apply to his life, so adults are focused on the immediate practical application. Remember, as a child, always hearing adults, teachers, parents, and neighbors tell you that *some day* you were going to need to know this? Well, now that you are an adult, *some day* is here! Adults in your class want to know the usefulness of a lesson for right now!

This does not mean, however, that lesson content is unimportant. Obviously, adults must first know the Bible well before they are able to apply it. Even so, teachers must keep a lesson geared towards the application. After all, that is the focus of the Bible, too—to teach us how to please God. Every Bible lesson, therefore, must also focus on how the Scripture passage applies to learners' everyday lives.

Adults are intrinsically motivated – Adults like to learn. Whereas educators employ external tools, such as awards and grades, to motivate children and youth (even college students) to learn, most adults are motivated by learning and the application of that learning. The adults who followed Jesus throughout the countryside and sought after his teaching were motivated intrinsically, by a desire to learn. Whereas youthful formal educational programs use rules, regulations, and awards to motivate participants to continue learning, adults participate mostly because they want to learn. Ask a child why he or she attends school and the most likely response will be that it is required. Ask a college student why he or she attends a college and the student will typically answer to get a degree. But then ask an adult why he or she participates in an educational program and he or she will probably give an explanation related to a specific goal to be achieved, the intrinsic value in learning, or an enjoyment of the learning activity itself and the social interaction it provides.[3] Adults overwhelmingly indicate that they participate in education for internal reasons—not to achieve external rewards.

Adults are self-directed learners – Children and youth are often dependent upon a teacher or leader to dictate to them what they need to learn and the curriculum to follow to accomplish their learning goals.

Adults can determine their own learning needs and objectives. In fact, adults often organize and complete their own learning projects. For example, an adult may be struggling with how to witness to his or her neighbor. That individual will read books on witnessing, study appropriate Bible passages, and talk with pastors and friends. Adults participate in self-directed learning activities almost every day.

In Bible learning in the church, adults are also self-directed. They know what their needs are and want to fulfill specific learning objectives. Because of their rich experience in learning activities, adults also often know what learning experiences will best help them achieve those learning objectives. While formal educators in children and youth educational programs plan curricular and learning activities *for* the participants, adult educators develop educational programs and learning events *with* the participants. Leaders and teachers of local church educational programs can utilize the self-directedness of adults to create learning opportunities that really help adults learn and grow in their faith and spiritual life. There are a number of ways in which adults can communicate their personal needs and learning goals. These goals can then be integrated into the church's educational planning to assure that the learning needs of adults are met. It is important that adults are also involved in the learning activities that will be implemented. In that sense they are helping to direct their learning and provide learning events that will be the most helpful.

Adults are experiential learners – You know all the old sayings: "You learn best by experience," "Experience is the best teacher," and "The best lessons in life are learned by experience." Well, it's true. Sam and Sylvia came to life when they were able to become involved with the lesson. All adults enter an educational experience with much previous experience and knowledge from which to draw. They also accomplish learning through experiencing it.

Think of what you've learned recently. Most likely, it was through an experience you had—either something you did, such as accomplishing a task around the house or completing a project at work, or a mental or spiritual exercise, such as doing daily devotions, reading a book, or participating in a discussion. Whatever it was, you, personally, experienced it and learned it. Even in an adult class or group setting, adults learn from experience. Information may be presented, but it is through the interaction on that information that learning occurs. Each individual adult must "experience" the learning objective in order for learning to occur. This is why participative, interactive classes are so important for adults.

Adults learn from each other – The greatest resource in any class of adults is not the textbook or the classroom or the teaching resources or even the teacher. Other than the Bible itself, the greatest resource for adult Bible learning is the adult class members themselves. As adults study together, believers can each share their Spirit-empowered illumination of God and His Word. Each can offer a wealth of experience, expertise, and knowledge to the group. Curtis was a prime example of this in the introduction to this chapter. The gifted teacher of adults, therefore, utilizes all the resources of the members of the group to achieve learning goals. The learning goals are achieved, therefore, not by what the teacher communicates but by the class members "teaching" each other.

Stop and think for a moment about the members of a group of adults in which you participate. Think about the expertise and experience of each member in that group. Sharing experiences is a tremendous resource for the members of that group. Adults benefit when they learn from each other.Teachers must seek to provide opportunities for this learning to occur.

Adults are critical thinkers – Maybe you have noticed that your adult learners are no longer satisfied with simplistic or clichéd explanations for complex issues. Many are seeking real answers to tough, nagging questions, such as, "Why does God allow pain and suffering?" or, "What makes Christianity so different from other religions?" Others are seeking to find a Christian view of contemporary ethical issues.

Developmentally, we learn that adults are improving in their ability to think independently and abstractly. They are able to consider multiple perspectives on an issue (see chapter seven). Key adult education theorists, such as Jack Mezirow and Paulo Freire structure their entire approach to adult learning around an adult's ability to critically reflect on his or her own underlying assumptions, biases, beliefs, and values.[4]

What does this mean for teachers? This means your adults will not be afraid to challenge your ideas or the ideas of other classmates. They will need mentally stimulating class sessions where they are encouraged to examine and question complex issues.

Adults are individuals – Although we can name some general characteristics of adult learners, there is no substitute for knowing *your* individual adult learners. They have different personalities, backgrounds, and abilities. They learn and think in different ways. Two prominent theories that capture these differences are the theories of learning styles and multiple intelligences.

Learning Styles

Based on personality, past learning experiences, and even cultural background, adults have developed preferences for how they like to learn. Many theorists believe that adults learn best when the teaching style matches their preferred learning style, although this is debated.

One educator, Bernice McCarthy, describes the four learning styles as follows:[5]

Innovative Learners (or Imaginative Learners) – Their favorite question is "Why do I need to learn this?" These learners seek personal meaning and engagement in the learning process, and they enjoy social interaction.

Analytic Learners – Their favorite question is "What do I need to know?" These learners seek facts, enjoy individual research, and are interested in what the experts say. They usually thrive in traditional, lecture-oriented classrooms.

Common Sense Learners – Their favorite question is "How does this work?" These learners seek relevance and usability and like to test out ideas for themselves in "real-life" settings.

Dynamic Learners – Their favorite question is "What can this become?" These are the creator-learners. They constantly follow their hunches to find new directions and possibilities in learning.

For optimum learning, McCarthy recommends that curriculum be designed to include each of these four learning styles. In this way, she says, students will have at least one part in the lesson where they will learn more successfully. They will also be challenged to learn in other styles.

Multiple Intelligences

The learners in your class will have strengths in several areas. Just look at the different careers they choose! You may have park rangers, musicians, mechanics, teachers, salespeople, and hairstylists all in one class. Howard Gardner was the first to introduce the theory of multiple intelligences, which included at least eight intellectual abilities that may not be measurable by standard IQ tests.[6] It is helpful to think of these as strengths in specific areas of learning. For example, some of your adult learners will be skilled at aspects of language, such as reading, writing, listening, and speaking (linguistic intelligence). Others will have exceptional musical or mathematical ability (musical intelligence and logical/mathematical intelligence). Still others will respond best to visual information (spatial intelligence) or activities that allow them to physically move around (bodily-kinesthetic intelligence). You will also have students who are especially wired to relationships. These students are exceptionally skilled at working with others (interpersonal intelligence) or at understanding themselves and knowing how to work best by themselves (intrapersonal intelligence). Finally, others are strong in recognizing and classifying the natural world (naturalist intelligence).

Most individuals possess skills in each of these learning areas to some extent, but they differ in skill levels and in unique combinations of strengths and weaknesses. It is important to be aware of these different strengths and to include them in lesson-planning, especially because adults often want help in their practical lives and ministry careers.

Summary

Adults are pragmatic, task-oriented, self-directed, experiential learners, who have different learning styles and strengths. So what does all of this mean to you as a teacher of an adult Bible class or Bible study group? First, it will definitely affect the role you play as a teacher. Since adults learn from each other and through experience, teachers of adults must resist the temptation to *tell* their class members what they want them to know and instead must provide opportunities for the adult participants to personally interact with the class objectives.

Second, it will require the use of a variety of methods, which may be different from the ones you have currently been using. You will need to use methods that are most in line with the characteristics of adult learning. You will also need to use different methods to address the various learning styles and strengths represented in your class.

Finally, it will require an attitude of appreciation. Rejoice in how God has created adult learners. Appreciate the unique contribution each adult learner makes to the class. This attitude will go far as you seek to nurture the adult learners in your class or group.

For Further Discussion

1. Think of the last time you learned something. How did you learn it? Compare your experience to the ingredients of adult learning from this chapter.

2. How would you teach the Bible to a class of adults who are pragmatic, task-oriented learners?

3. Brainstorm, with other adult teachers, how you might teach John 4 to a class of adults, being sure to give attention to all the ingredients of adult learning identified in this chapter.

4. Brainstorm, with other adult teachers, how to provide opportunities for adult class members to learn from the other participants in the class.

Notes

1. Eduard C. Lindeman, *The Meaning of Adult Education* (New York: New Republic, 1926), 3.

2. See Malcom S. Knowles, *The Modern Practice of Adult Education: From Pedagogy to Andragogy*, 2d ed. (New York: Cambridge Books, 1980).

3. This is based on research done by C. O. Houle, *The Inquiring Mind* (Madison: University of Wisconsin Press, 1961).

4. See Jack Mezirow, *Learning as Transformation* (San Francisco: Jossey-Bass, Inc., 2000) and Paulo Friere, *Education for Critical Consciousness* (New York: Seabury Press, 1973).

5. Bernice McCarthy, *About Teaching: 4Mat in the Classroom.* (Wauconda, Ill.: About Learning, Inc., 2000). For a Christian perspective of learning styles, see Marlene LeFever, *Learning Styles: Reaching Everyone God Gave You to Teach* (Colorado Springs: David C. Cook, 1995).

6. Howard Gardner, *Multiple Ingelligences: The Theory in Practice* (New York: Basic Books, 1993). Gardner added his eighth intelligence, the naturalist intelligence in later writings.

3-C Teachers of Adults

~ 3 ~

Teachers of adults are the key ingredient to adult learning, biblical literacy, and spiritual growth. Remember Maria from the first chapter? When Betty asked her how she taught her adult class, she responded that she "facilitates" the class. Through her qualities and skills as a teacher, Maria was the driving force behind the learning that was taking place. She was the one mainly responsible for creating an opportunity for adults to grow closer to their Savior, to learn from each other, and to discover God's truth in a personal way. The role of the teacher in successful adult learning cannot be underestimated.

The 3-C Teacher

What are the characteristics of a successful adult Bible teacher? First, a person must have a personal and growing relationship with Jesus Christ. He or she must be a dedicated Christian. Beyond this initial requirement, what are the required qualities and skills to effectively lead an adult class? It is helpful to think of these non-negotiables as the 3-C's of adult teaching.

Compassion – The most common Greek word translated into our English Bibles as "compassion" (*splagknon*) describes an inward compulsion to reach out to help someone in need. It is the ability to feel someone else's pain in your heart. Most of the fourteen occurrences of the word *compassion* in the gospels refer to this virtue as it was expressed through the life and ministry of Christ. It was the compassion of Jesus that moved Him to pursue needy people. Likewise, it was that very same compassion that caused needy people to pursue Him. Sincere compassion is magnetic!

Jesus not only cared about the people, His compassion made Him do something about it. In Mark 6:30–44 we read that one day, when Jesus was especially tired and needed rest, He saw the people in need and helped them. Even though He was tired, Jesus' compassion made Him reach out to others. Likewise, teachers with the compassion of Jesus will reach out and help their class members as well.

Jesus also demonstrated His compassion in His intense attention to individuals. His interactions with people show us His ability to discern a person's heart and his or her unique spiritual needs or struggles. His response was often tailor-made to different individuals or groups. Look at the different ways He lovingly spoke the truth to the woman at the well (John 4:1–42), the rich young ruler (Matt. 19:16–22), or the Pharisees (Matt. 15:2–3). As teachers, we must also show this same discernment and individualized response to the adults in our care.

Being compassionate also means being a good shepherd. Jesus describes Himself as the Good Shepherd who lays down His life for His sheep (Jn. 10:15). He knows each of His followers by name, and His followers know Him. This loving Shepherd is committed not to lose any that the Father has given Him (Jn. 10:28; 17:12). As teachers we must also be willing to "lay down our life" in many ways for the flock God has entrusted to us. We must know our adults by name and keep watch over their spiritual well-being.

Perhaps no other spiritual attribute than compassion better defines what is generally meant when someone speaks of a Christlike person. Adults in this modern age are still attracted to leaders with this quality.

Content – The most influential teachers in Scripture all possessed a great knowledge of the Bible. Look at the teaching ministries of Jesus and of the apostle Paul! They had tremendous knowledge of the Scriptures and were able to use that knowledge in their teaching. There's an old saying: "Teaching something you don't know is as meaningless as coming back from somewhere you've never been!" Bible teachers, first, need to know the Bible. Then they can teach it to others.

But have no fear! Knowing the Bible does not mean you have to be a Bible expert. In fact, there will most likely be men and women you teach who know more about the Bible than you do. It does mean, however, that you need to know enough so you can ensure your class is based on biblical truth. Even when you are facilitating a discussion, it is your responsibility that biblical truth is clearly communicated and understood by class members.

Knowledge of the Bible should include three areas:

1. *Overall Bible knowledge:* How the parts relate to each other.
2. *Theology:* What the Bible means for the world.
3. *Understanding of the passage:* Comprehension of the context.

Collaboration – Once again we return to the Master Teacher. Volumes have been written to document the teaching skills of Jesus. His ability to teach eternal truths to men and women of all social strata is unmatched. His mastery of instructional methods, some of which were nontraditional in his day, still baffles educators. His expertise in designing lessons that move toward a specifically predetermined life response still stands as the ideal by which curriculum planning is evaluated.

The key to Jesus' teaching was the ways in which He involved His learners. He was a master at asking questions, using illustrations that related directly to the lives of the people, and then providing real life learning experiences. The same principles apply to Bible learning today. Although it is easiest to "tell" people biblical truth, we all learn best by experience, by interacting with the truth on our own. The effective Bible teacher, therefore, is actually one who collaborates with students in the learning process. This means that the teacher is more of a facilitator, creating opportunities for class members to learn the Bible on their own and through interaction with others in the class. He or she is not "a sage on the stage, but a guide on the side." This involves the ability to facilitate learning activities, individual study of the Bible, and group discussions to help class members learn and achieve the class learning objectives.

Collaboration with learners is especially important in the adult class. Adult learners have a wealth of knowledge, experience, and expertise to share. The collective wisdom of the adults in the group will almost always be greater than the knowledge of the teacher alone. Experienced teachers of adults are not threatened by this. They are willing to take the humble position of co-learner, allowing themselves to learn from others in the class and valuing this learning. Overall, the adult class or small group is a place for collaboration in learning. Through skilled facilitation, the adult teacher creates a setting where participants join together and collaborate on the journey of discovering truth.

The Gift of Teaching

In His infinite wisdom Jesus has designed that His teaching ministry would be continued after His departure. The angels were not commissioned with the task. The "super saints" of Old Testament history were not resurrected to finish the job. God has gifted farmers, mechanics, housewives, salesmen, and other ordinary people and assigned them with this duty.

The ability to excel in the teaching of biblical truths is a spiritual gift, empowered by the Holy Spirit. Those who possess this gift will demonstrate varying degrees of teaching ability. In many cases, gifted teachers will not have developed their gifts well enough to achieve optimum effectiveness. Biblical teaching may be rooted in a gift, but it becomes an art only as it is nurtured through experience and training.

If you are unsure whether or not you have the spiritual gift of teaching, here are some practical pointers:

1. Ask God to give you inner confirmation regarding what spiritual gift(s) you have been given.
2. Ask two or three of your closest Christian friends for their feedback regarding the spiritual gift(s) they see in you.
3. Talk with those who have the gift of teaching regarding their own discovery of their gift(s).
4. Volunteer for teaching opportunities. God will confirm your giftedness as you begin to develop the gift.
5. Remember that a spiritual gift is just that—a gift! We should gratefully receive and use them.

The 3-C's in Practice

The most effective teachers of adults possess to some degree all of the 3-C's of compassion, content, and collaboration. However, if you struck out in one or two of these areas, take heart! The history of adult Bible teaching is replete with exceptions. Remember, the gift of teaching becomes art only as it is nurtured through experience and training.

So what can you do to develop the 3-C's? For a motivated teacher, each of the 3-C's can be developed prayerfully through study, training, and experience.

Deficiencies in the 3-C's can also be overcome by utilizing complementary skills possessed by other members of the class. The greatest weakness any teacher can have is the weakness of not admitting his or her weakness, or having acknowledged it, not being willing to seek help. The best teachers of adults seek help from members of the class through advice and coaching and by involving the class members in class leadership opportunities. One effective way to make use of the complementary skills of class members is through team teaching.

Team Teaching and the 3-C's

Team teaching is when two or more persons cooperatively engage in the task of teaching through planning, implementing, and fostering a climate and the accompanying experiences that encourage learning to occur. The end result is a teaching session that reflects the collective teaching wisdom of the entire team. Teaching motivation is enhanced because the entire team feels a sense of lesson ownership.

There are many benefits of team teaching to teachers, their class participants, and the entire adult educational program. First, a teaching team can capitalize upon the strengths of individual teachers and work around their weaknesses. An effective teaching team should consist of teachers with complementary 3-C strengths.

Second, through team teaching, new teachers are able to develop their skills and become integrated into a teaching role. As potential teachers in the class are spotted, they are given increasing amounts of responsibility and guidance by current "mentor" teachers until they are ready to share more of the team teaching load.

Additional strengths of team teaching are a higher quality of the teaching-learning experience due to input from several teachers; a "fellowship of the gospel" as team teachers meet regularly to study, plan, and pray together; a decrease of the teacher "burn out" factor; and a variety of teacher backgrounds, styles, and personalities to better relate with diverse adult students in the class. Perhaps the greatest strength of team teaching is the growth and multiplication of classes as new teachers are continually developed! Although there can be potential personality conflicts and scheduling conflicts among team teachers, the benefits to team teaching far outweigh the difficulties. It is a viable option for improving your impact and effectiveness as a 3-C teacher of adults.

Summary

Teachers should honestly evaluate their strengths in light of the 3-C's of teaching adults. They should plan to take maximum advantage of their strengths, while seeing their deficiencies as challenges to overcome by personal effort or by seeking the assistance of other class members or teachers with counterbalancing skills. The most important lesson to be learned is that it was God who made us with our abilities, or lack of them. He does not expect or desire for us to replicate the ministry of other teachers who have been given a different set of strengths and weaknesses. Team teaching is an excellent method to provide complementary skills in teaching, personality type, and perspectives, as well as develop new teachers.

Church leaders should recruit adult teachers and teams of teachers with the 3-C's in mind. As tempting as it may be, they should avoid filling adult teaching positions with people who lack compassion, content, and collaboration in teaching. In doing so, the class and the unqualified teacher will be spared a lot of frustration, and learning will be enhanced.

For Further Discussion

1. Think of the best adult teacher you have ever had. Which of the 3-C's (compassion, content, or collaboration) did this person possess? If this person possessed two or more of these traits, which was the most apparent and attractive of the characteristics?

2. What can you learn about the gift of teaching from the following passages? Romans 12:1–8; 1 Corinthians 12–14; Ephesians 4:7–13; and 1 Peter 4:7–11.

3. Evaluate your own abilities in light of the 3-C's. Better yet, ask a close friend who has observed you as a teacher to do this for you. What can and should you learn from this analysis?

4. In your estimation, what would be the single greatest advantage of team teaching to you, as an adult teacher? What would be the most difficult hurdle for you to overcome in implementing a team teaching format?

5. Think of potential teachers in your class or Bible study group. What are some ways in which they could become involved in leadership of the class? Map out a plan in which you could help them grow to be an experienced teacher.

Purposes of Adult Classes

~ 4 ~

There is sometimes a temptation for adult teachers to take on a "lone ranger" mentality about their adult class or group. They and their members see their class as a separate entity that in many ways is independent of the larger church body. Focusing their efforts on creating "the best adult class ever" or "the most dynamic women's small group," they miss the larger picture of how their adult class fits into the purposes of the local church.

Most church leaders agree upon the biblical purposes for the church. These include worship, edification (instruction and fellowship), and evangelism. So where do adult classes or groups fit in? Adult classes or groups are agencies that primarily assist the local church in achieving the purposes of evangelism and edification. Within these larger purposes, adult classes serve four basic functions as an entry point, an assimilation network, a shepherding outpost, and a ministry mobilization unit.

Entry Point

Can you imagine a church building without any doors? Just suppose that a local congregation launched an impressive building program. No expense was spared in the process of creating an environment that would set a worshipful tone for the corporate assembly. Suppose, however, that there were no doors! What ministry value would those beautiful buildings have without entry points?

The most important entry points to a church, however, are not the physical openings into the building. As attractive and inviting as these entrances may be, the real entry points for a church are those ministry programs that establish a welcoming relationship with people outside of the church's ongoing fellowship. Throughout their history, the educational classes have been a major entry point for local churches. Adult classes usually fall into one of three categories:

Closed Classes

Every church has classes that are not open to new members. Various church boards or Bible class leaders and teachers will meet for a group Bible study. Ladies' and men's classes, as well as age-group classes, are closed to those who do not meet those restrictions. Closed classes are not entry points. It is important for many of these classes to remain closed in order to help build unity and achieve the class objectives. Not all the adult classes and Bible study groups, however, should be closed to new members.

Passive Entry Points

Some adult classes and Bible study groups are open, but only to "walk ins" who visit the church and look for an adult class or Bible study to join. Visitors who are actively seeking a point of entry into the life of the church body can find it through these classes as long as they are willing to take some initiative to locate the class for themselves. Passive entry point classes make a genuine attempt to receive visitors into the fellowship once they arrive.

Active Entry Points

An active entry point class is one that has a genuine sense of mission for reaching out to new participants. These classes are not content with a "come to us" approach to ministry. They are entry points with red carpets that roll out into the church vestibule and beyond, embracing the surrounding community. Prospective members may be those who have never visited the church, those who have visited the church, or those who are church members but are not active in adult educational programs.

Assimilation Network

Members need to be assimilated into the local church congregation. Visitors are often allowed, even "welcomed," to attend church functions but are not easily able to become full-fledged members of the group. In larger churches or growing churches, it is not unusual to hear comments such as, "We just feel lost" or "Our church does not seem as friendly as it used to be." If the leadership fails to develop a successful procedure for absorbing new people into the church body, a loss of members or a plateau in church attendance is inevitable.

There is, however, a positive correlation between the number of relationships a person has and the degree of his or her commitment to and continuing participation in a group. Fifty new members who remained active in church six months after joining were compared with fifty new members who dropped out during the same period. Those who continued as active members had made an average of more than seven new friends during the six months. Those who were not assimilated into the ongoing fellowship made less than two such friendships.[1]

Adult classes and groups are extremely important as assimilating networks. Church members and visitors who sense they truly "belong" to a smaller group within the church are less likely to feel lost or bothered by a large church atmosphere in the worship services. By carefully planned effort, church leaders and adult class leaders can help class members broaden their bonding, from the class to the entire church body. Interclass activities, socials involving multiple adult small groups, visits of church leaders to adult classes, and an ongoing emphasis on the integrative relationship of adult classes and the total church are helpful.

Shepherding Outpost

There is no better term than "pastor" or "shepherd" to describe the ministry role that effective adult teachers fulfill as they nurture a body of believers. They help to feed the people the proper nourishing diet of biblical truths. They guard and protect the flock by exhorting them to live by biblical wisdom. Lovingly, they care for the needs of hurting students. As shepherds, these teachers assist the pastor by serving as undershepherds over a subgroup within the larger congregation. Their adult Bible class or group serves as a a shepherding outpost, which provides at least four basic ministries to adults:

1. Biblical Teaching – The first and primary task of a teacher is to teach—and to teach the Bible! Society today is suffering from extreme biblical illiteracy. The pastor cannot be expected to function as the only instructor of the Bible. The schools cannot be expected to teach adults the Bible; relatively few adults have the opportunity to study the Bible in a college class. The task of eradicating biblical illiteracy is given to the teachers of adult classes and the leaders of adult Bible study groups. These Bible-based adult ministries can be excellent complements and supplements to a pastor's pulpit ministry.

The second "C" relates to Bible knowledge, but the third "C" relates to teaching skill, the facilitation of group learning. The task of an adult Bible teacher is not necessarily to present his or her knowledge of the Bible; rather, it is to ultimately help the adult class participants to learn the Bible for themselves. As a teacher facilitates the learning of adults and encourages a spirit of collaboration in learning, adults will learn deep Bible truths. Remember, if the adults in your class have not learned, you have not taught.

2. Fellowship – The word *fellowship* immediately conjures up memories of "fuzzy" warm gatherings, usually in some way associated with food and fun. Fellowship (from the Greek word *koinonia*) is more than social interaction, however. It is a deep spiritual bond first with the Son of God and then with each other (1Cor. 1:9; 1 John 1:6–7). True fellowship is sharing together, rejoicing with those who rejoice, and mourning with those who mourn (Rom. 12:15). This type of fellowship does not just happen. It is the result of the Spirit-filled efforts of every participant, led by the example of the teacher. A major focus of every adult class and Bible study group must be to build this fellowship, and time should be invested every time the group meets to achieving this purpose.

As society outside the church grows increasingly impersonal, classes that exhibit such sincere care are sure to appeal to a growing number of adults. In fact, research confirms many adults seek out a learning opportunity because of the social interaction it provides.[2]

3. Healing – The healing ministry of an adult class should not focus on physical infirmities alone. The kind of healing that is most needed in adult classes and Bible study groups focuses on spiritual and emotional needs.

The need for spiritual and emotional help today is unprecedented. Pastors and professional counselors have experienced a tremendous demand for counseling services. Support groups, which meet on a regular basis and allow group members to receive mutual emotional support, are one way to effectively meet this demand. Much emotional and spiritual healing can be accomplished through the support and encouragement of members of an adult class or Bible study group.

Healing should be a major purpose of adult classes. In addition to time being invested for this purpose at group meetings, a wise teacher will be sensitive to the needs of the individuals in the group and the group as a whole. Teachers must occasionally take time outside of class to meet the needs of adult members as situations arise. They must also know when to refer certain problems to professionally trained Christian counselors.

4. Equipping – The ultimate success of a class is not measured in terms of the class size or the retention rate of its members. The desired end of adult ministry is training adults for leadership and service (Eph. 4). Teachers want to see members who have been equipped through sound teaching and exhortation move out into areas of Christian service, maybe even beginning adult classes of their own. A constant turnover of class membership is desired if it is prompted by a motivation to put Bible learning into practice.

Equipping for service should be an announced purpose of every adult class or Bible study group. Decrease in class enrollment, when caused by an increase in the church's ministry workforce, is a self-effacing but Christ exalting act (John 3:30). The equipping cycle can be further encouraged by an emphasis upon the implementation of spiritual gifts. Perhaps it is even wise to teach a series of lessons, from time to time, which deals with various facets of ministry.

Ministry Mobilization Unit

Adult classes and Bible study groups can serve as units of ministry "person-power" to tackle two different types of tasks. First, classes may focus upon ministry projects for which they take the sole responsibility. For example, a class may assume the regular duty of organizing or leading services at a rescue mission, nursing home, or local jail. There are also many possibilities for short-term projects. Adults may offer to help individuals within the group move into a new home. Another class might take a collection to help needy individuals within the class. Other possible ideas are fixing someone's home, raising funds for a particular missionary need, or planning a farewell reception for class members who are relocating.

Second, different adult classes and Bible study groups can be asked to help accomplish various church-wide duties. Some large tasks can be broken up into manageable pieces and assigned to adult groups. Preparation for a church missions conference can be accomplished in this manner. Follow up of visitors to the church could also be done through the appropriate adult classes and Bible study groups. Churches commonly assign the care of members who are ill, those who are in a state of financial need, or others who need special attention to the adult classes of which they are members.

Summary

Adult classes are important parts of the church that contribute to the larger goals of edification and evangelism. These groups achieve significant functions from helping persons find an entry point into the church fellowship; to assimilating them into the congregation; to shepherding them through biblical instruction, fellowship, healing, and equipping; and then mobilizing them into ministry. Adult Bible teachers must seek to achieve all these class functions. Some of the class functions will be achieved over time, and some will be achieved each time the class meets, providing a significant ministry in the lives of adult members.

For Further Discussion

1. Evaluate each adult class or Bible study group in your church to see if it is closed, passive, or active. What can be done to increase the number of active entry point classes?
2. Discuss why people are or are not being effectively assimilated into your church body.
3. Study John 10:1-18. What principles of shepherding from this passage can be applied to teaching an adult Bible class?
4. What are areas of ministry mobilization in which your class or group could participate?

Notes

1. Charles Arn, Donald McGavran, and Win Arn, *Growth: A New Vision for the Sunday School* (Pasadena: Church Growth Press, 1980), 95.
2. This information is based on a study done by P. J. Fujita-Starck, "Motivations and Characteristics of Adult Students," *Adult Education Quarterly* 47, no. 1 (1996): 29–40.

Building Adult Community

~ 5 ~

It is helpful to think of your adult class or group as a microcosm. *Micro* means "little," and *cosm* means "world." Thus, a microcosm is literally a "little world" that serves as a miniature model of a larger world. The adult Bible class or group is a microcosm of the local church and the even larger body of Christ. Therefore, the description of the body of Christ presented in Ephesians 4 serves as a blueprint for adult education leaders as well.

These verses tell us that the ultimate goal of adult Bible class ministry is spiritual growth. This growth is centered on Christ and is accomplished through the speaking of the truth and the interdependent workings of class members, all within a framework of love. If the adult class is a true church microcosm, then an atmosphere of loving, mutual edification should also prevail. This is true, biblical community. It is the sense of spiritual oneness that is ultimately achieved by the Holy Spirit's ministry in the lives of class members. Adult community has been developed successfully when every member feels that he or she is a wanted, necessary, and functioning part of the group, a microcosm of the body of Christ.

Though adult teachers may understand the concept of the adult class as a microcosm of the body of Christ, unless the class membership also understands and acts on the concept, little progress will be realized toward the Ephesians 4 ideal. This type of community is the result of the prayerful efforts of every participant, led by the example of the teacher. A focus on community-building is essential to an effective Bible teaching ministry.

There are at least five ways that time can be utilized in order to encourage the adult class or group to develop a deep sense of community. These community facilitator times are conversational time, get acquainted time, prayer and share time, sing time, and outside of class time.

Conversational Time

This is the informal time set aside for class members to engage in casual conversations. This is not wasted time, but time well spent. Adults learn valuable information about each other in casual interactions, and it is important they first know each other on a casual, friendly level before deeper community can develop. Conversational time can be either planned as pre-meeting time or as a scheduled part of the class time. It may also begin as a pre-meeting activity and continue on into the actual class session.

Pre-meeting conversational time is a noble concept that has one catch to it—it requires people to arrive at the class early. For some early birds, this is no problem. Other members will need some encouragement. Perhaps a coffeepot or snack table will provide an effective incentive.

Conversational time is not limited to pre-meeting time. One class takes a five minute "M and M" (mix and mingle) intermission shortly after the class begins. Class members are encouraged to stand up, move around, pour another cup of coffee, and greet several other people, especially visitors. This activity loosens up the group, encourages visitor assimilation, provides an active break, and allows latecomers a conversational time that they may have missed.

Get Acquainted Time

Every adult teacher should be haunted by the prospect of an adult visitor or class member leaving a class as anonymous as they were when they entered it. For a teacher to remember the names of his or her class members and visitors will take some effort. For other class members to learn these same names is an even greater challenge. Teachers cannot be content to leave this responsibility with the class. Except for the few gregarious members of the class, most members will not make any special effort to become acquainted with other regular attendees, much less visitors.

Teachers should seek to implement many means of increasing the name recognition and recall within the class. In larger classes certain regular members can be distributed throughout the classroom for the purpose of meeting visitors, getting to know them, and introducing them to the entire class at a designated time.

Ideally, get-acquainted activities are integrated into the instructional objectives of the lesson. For example, during a lesson about Peter walking on the water, class members could be asked to share an experience in which they were required to step out in faith. This accomplishes a double-purpose: adult community is being built among the class members and learning is occurring.

Prayer and Share Time

Community life will not be developed without the essential elements of corporate prayer and praise. This is true Christian fellowship, or *koinonia*, when believers share common experiences and expressions of their faith and unite spiritually in relationship to Christ and to each other. Every class or group session should allow time for members to share prayer burdens and for members to pray for these requests together. In many large churches the most significant opportunity for meaningful corporate prayer will come through the adult classes and Bible study groups.

The prayer and share time is not only for prayer but also for praise and mutual ministry. Members are encouraged to share special blessings, Scripture verses, or answered prayers that they have experienced recently. This builds up the faith of those who listen. Time should also be allowed for class members to minister to each other, using such gifts of encouragement, exhortation, mercy, and wisdom. It can also be a time of confession of sin and emotional and spiritual healing as class members receive forgiveness from the Lord and others (James 5:15-16). These times reap eternal dividends as they help build community in the adult class or group.

Sing Time

Group singing can create a powerful spiritual bond in your adult group. The use and frequency of singing will vary with the size of the class, the classroom setting, the availability and ability of a song leader within the class, and the degree of the group's interest in and ability for singing.

There are many ways to make music a part of adult classes. Some classes use musical instruments such as the piano or guitar to accompany them as they sing. The guitar has a special appeal to most adults and seems to be well suited for the size of most classes. Other classes use sound track accompaniment or sing a cappella. Whatever the method, it is important that members can follow along with songbooks or songsheets, overhead transparencies, or Powerpoint slides. Be sure to secure necessary copyright permissions for these items. Special music performances can be provided occasionally or regularly in certain classes. In this way members are given the opportunity to minister to their class through music.

Corporate singing does more than contribute to worship. It unites the hearts of class members and assists in creating community. Some Christian songs, by the very nature of the words and the tone of the music, create a unifying group effect. Teachers may want to select a few such songs and use them frequently. Perhaps the most effective use of music is incorporating musical presentations and corporate singing into the lesson as a reinforcement of a certain point. By using popular contemporary Christian songs in the class or group teaching session, the lesson is reinforced when class members hear the same songs on the radio or on CD's during the week.

Outside of Class Time

True class community life, as well as the full growth and learning benefits of participating in an adult Bible class, should not and cannot be confined to class meetings. If class community and learning is to fully occur, out-of-class activities will be necessary. Not only do these activities foster community-building but they also allow members to use their spiritual gifts to serve each other in various ways.

Four major kinds of extracurricular adult class activities can contribute to class community life and personal and spiritual growth: social activities, caring ministries, outreach efforts, and accountability or care groups.

Social Activities

Well-planned social activities create a strong sense of synergy and cohesiveness within the entire group. Social activities also contribute to meaningful relationships as members increasingly relate on both a spiritual and social level. To produce these benefits, an adult class social activity program requires much thought and work. Some factors to consider are cost, timing, appropriateness, variety, and the amount of effort required to make it happen. Four basic guiding principles should underlie the whole process.

1. Keep the focus on building community – Events should allow time for casual conversations or a more formal sharing time when the whole group can interact. Interactive activities, such as potluck and progressive dinners, ice cream socials, chili cook-offs, hayrides, and other outside activities, are preferred to less-interactive activities, like sporting events, concerts, and movies. Less-interactive activities can, however, be preceded or followed by more interactive activities such as a dinner or dessert.

2. Social activities should take place on a regular basis – Each class needs to decide its own frequency rate. Usually three or four major activities per year are a minimum. Other smaller events can be planned to fill the gaps between larger events.

3. Responsibilities for planning social activities should be shared – The practice of selecting an activity committee or coordinator for a year at a time is a workable plan. Another idea is to rotate the responsibility of planning social events. Social event planning offers abundant opportunities for serving-gifted class members to exercise gifts of administration or hospitality.

4. Make use of technology in social activities – In addition to the obvious opportunities available through the use of the telephone, such as telephone trees, prayer chains, and so forth, the computer provides excellent options for adult community building. A group email list can be created so that group members can be in constant communication. Upcoming events, prayer needs and updates, and even learning activities related to previous or upcoming lessons can be communicated through this group email list. Some churches establish a web site for the various adult classes and Bible study groups. This provides even more opportunities for interaction through message boards, chat rooms, and information dissemination.

Caring Ministries

Wounded travelers are all around us. Maybe we cannot respond to all of them, but we cannot afford to miss those who have committed themselves to the care of our Bible classes. At least three types of needs are found among the members of our adult classes:

1. Health needs – In larger churches, adults may identify more closely with their adult class than with the church as a whole. Consequently, one of the first individuals called in times of crisis is an adult Bible teacher. However, once the initial shock of the news has passed, these teachers and their classes may forget the wounded traveler. The hurting member should not be left to recover alone.

Not all health needs are physical. The emotional afflictions caused by divorce, rebellious children, and the death of loved ones also demand the attention and care of sincere modern day Good Samaritans with gifts of mercy and compassion.

2. *Benevolence needs* – There may be times when members of the class are struggling to meet basic life needs—such as food, housing, and employment. Although most churches help the needy through benevolent offerings and other funds, adults in need often feel most comfortable asking for help from the close community that exists in their adult Bible classes. Some adult classes take a collection for members when special needs arise. They may also provide members with special meals, offer a warm place to stay, or suggest opportunities to find employment.

3. *Help needs* – In Galatians 6:2, Paul says, "Bear ye one another's burdens." The word translated "burden" in this verse denotes a burdensome weight that presses on a person physically or that makes a heavy demand on one's resources, material or spiritual. When the weight of any kind of burden becomes more than an individual Christian can bear, other Christians fulfill the law of Christ by helping him or her with the load. It is important for class members to become aware of each other's burdens and to offer a practical helping hand when needed. Class service projects, such as raking leaves for a widow or helping a family move are ideas to bear others' burdens.

It is also important for the group to be focused outside the needs of the immediate group to the larger church body, the community, and even the world. The adult class can be a powerhouse for the Gospel as it mobilizes a group of people to serve Christ in tangible ways. Possible ideas are painting the church building, serving food at a local homeless shelter, taking class mission trips to help a church-supported missionary, and making prayer commitments to church leaders and missionaries.

Outreach Efforts

If the class or group is open to new members, intentional outreach efforts should take place. Effective adult class outreach begins with a clear focus concerning contact targets. A careful selection of outreach methods and means is a second prerequisite. Adult classes commonly use four means of contacting their outreach targets: home visits, telephone calls, mail, and email. Contact targets and outreach means need to be woven into a systematic and comprehensive outreach strategy. Three likely contact targets for adult classes are new prospects, class visitors, and absentee class members.

1. New prospects – Someone in the church should be responsible for funneling adult class prospects to the leaders of the class best suited to the individual or individuals. The most likely candidates for membership in adult Bible classes are people who express an interest in the church. Visitor's cards collected in the worship services are a prime source of leads. Parents of children who attend the Sunday school, a club program, Vacation Bible School, or a weekday program are also good possibilities. Spiritual counseling contacts made by the pastor or other staff personnel should be pursued by adult classes as well.

The most natural, but frequently neglected, source of new prospects is the network of personal relationships of each current member of the class. These could be family members, neighbors, friends, or those they meet through common interests, such as hobbies or sporting events.

2. Class visitors – The most obvious place to start in building a class ministry is with the adults who have visited the class. A system of collecting and recording information about visitors is essential. Many classes use a visitor's form to gather the information and a notebook or computer to record it for a permanent file.

Turning visitors into regular class members is largely dependent upon two actions the class takes. First, visitors should be considered class members as soon they begin attending. Second, several contacts should be made with the visitor following the class as soon as possible. These contacts can be made by telephone, by mail or email, or in person.

3. Absentee class members – The class absentee list should be evaluated often to determine which members were absent and what effort, if any, should be taken to contact them. A class attendance book or computerized program can be used for keeping records of class enrollment and attendance. Record systems are only effective when they are used regularly and wisely as a basis for contacting visitors and absentees.

Accountability or Care Groups

Class relationships are reinforced as they carry over into everyday life. Pairs or subgroups can be formed that keep in contact during the week for the development of close relationships, prayer, mutual care and support, spiritual accountability, and further discussion and application of the weekly Bible lesson. If face-to-face contact is not possible, these groups can talk on the phone or conduct "cyber-space" discussions through email messages and chat rooms.

Summary

No adult Bible teacher should apologize for devoting significant time to building adult community! It is an important goal of adult classes and Bible study group ministry. In fact, in many churches, the adult educational groups are the only opportunities for close adult community. The building of adult community, the ministering of adults to each other, and the learning and applying of biblical truth all begin during the class session and continue throughout the week. Adult community can be built in at least four ways during actual class time: conversational time, get-acquainted time, prayer and share time, and sing time. However, the real impact of an adult Bible class or group, just like the real impact of a Bible sermon, takes place outside the structured session. Most of adult community is built in-between class sessions through social activities, caring ministries, outreach, and accountability groups. In today's technological age, it is even easier for class members to stay connected throughout the week with email, telephone, and chat rooms.

For Further Discussion

1. Other than those listed in the chapter, can you think of other activities that build adult class community?
2. What are the benefits of community-building to Bible learning? How do they mutually enhance each other?
3. Describe how the different spiritual gifts can be used in your class. How can you provide more opportunities to class members to use their gifts in your class ministry?
4. Discuss: Of the four types of out-of-class activities, which is most frequently done well? Which of these types of activities is most needed in the average adult class? Why?
5. List the "wounded travelers" that have had some relationship with your adult group over the past few years. Evaluate the response of your class to the challenge of helping these hurting people.

Designing Adult Bible Learning

~ 6 ~

"Wasn't that a great class?" exclaimed Debbie exuberantly as she walked out into the cold, crisp winter air.

Marlene was excited, too. "He is such a great teacher!" she added with a shrill in her voice, matching the chill of the night air outside.

But Lisa wasn't so sure. "I agree that Martin is a very interesting teacher, and I love his stories as much as anyone," Lisa began, "but, you know, I really don't know if I learned anything. Did you two?"

Her question stopped Debbie and Marlene dead in their tracks. As usual, they had really enjoyed the class. They laughed and cried and listened, but they had to admit they couldn't really put their finger on anything they had learned. In fact, now that Lisa had mentioned it, they were pretty passive in the class. They just listened.

Debbie remembered that Martin always commented about how much he had learned during the week preparing the lesson. He always seemed so excited about everything he had learned and was anxious to tell them about it. Debbie remembered feeling actually jealous. She wished she could have had some of that excitement, too. It was almost as if Martin was depriving her of the joy of learning. He was making it too easy for them. She was sure Martin remembered everything he had learned during the week. Maybe if she had the same experience she would remember more about the Bible, too.

The job of a Bible teacher, or any teacher, is to help the class participants learn. Actually, the teacher is working himself or herself out of a job. The teacher's goal is to be so successful in helping the class participants learn that they will be able to continue learning on their own, without the teacher's help.

How exactly, though, is that done? How does a teacher help the participants to learn? The first step is to not work so hard. Just as a parent is not doing his or her children any favors by completing their homework for them, so a teacher is not helping his or her class members by giving them all the answers or all the information. One adult teacher put it this way: "I have the class members tell me what I want them to know." This statement shows the role of the teacher as one who enables others to be self-learners. Consider the following steps to designing a Bible lesson that enables adults to be self-learners.

Setting Learning Goals

The best lesson preparation begins, literally, weeks before the class or group meets. The first question every teacher must ask before preparing to teach or lead an adult Bible group is: "What do my class members need to get out of this?" And the second question is: "What is the best way for them to accomplish that?"

Question number one requires a knowledge of the general needs, expressed and unexpressed, that exist within the group. It is important first to understand the spiritual needs of every Christian adult: to become more like Christ, to read and understand the Bible, to develop godly character, and so on. It is also crucial to understand the basic developmental needs of the adult age groups represented in the class (see chapter seven). Just as important, though, is to understand the current needs felt by the individual class members. This results from spending time with the group members.

Discovery of needs can take place in class during informal conversational times and even by paying close attention to the comments that are made during group discussions or the shared prayer requests. It can also take place in direct discussion by simply inviting class members to share their learning needs with you or with the group. Finally, it takes place as you, the teacher, spend time with adults outside of class, walking alongside them in life.

Once the needs of the adult group members have been established, goals for the learning experience can be set. It is often helpful to start off new adult groups with a discussion of the common goals adults would like to accomplish in their time together, whether it will extend for a weekend retreat, a quarter, or a year. Looking at these broad class or group goals, the teacher can then create goals for individual lessons and units. A unit is a lesson series unified by a common emphasis. A well-planned unit will have an overall unit aim. Although individual lessons within the unit will each have their own aims, all of the lessons will contribute to achieving the broader unit aim.

When creating goals, it is important to remember that learning does not just involve an increase in content knowledge but a change in understanding, attitudes, and behaviors as well. You are looking for life change in learners that affects their total person! All lesson planning should be made with this larger goal in mind.

Planning The Bible Lesson

Once we have answered the question, "What do my class members need to get out of this?" we move to the second question, "What is the best way for them to accomplish that?" Notice this question is not "What is the best way to present the material?" or "How can the teacher accomplish that?" Rather, we want to find the best way for adult learners to get what they need out of the lesson. They will be doing the work of learning; the teacher is only setting the stage for the work of learning to be accomplished. The three parts of the lesson you will need to plan are the lesson approach, the lesson development (or Bible study), and the lesson application.

The Lesson Approach

In the typical adult class or Bible study, opening activities and the Bible lesson are separated by an unabridged chasm. Class members find themselves casually talking and joking with friends, perhaps becoming acquainted with visitors, filling a plate with snacks, or joining in the group singing. Then it happens! The teacher begins the lesson and abruptly everything changes. Smiling faces become serious and talking voices stop. Adult minds shift gears to focus on the assigned topic for the day.

Instead of making the big leap across the chasm from opening activities to the Bible lesson, why not ease the transition with interactive, but lesson introducing, methods? Curriculum publishers use various names to refer to this part of the lesson. These include "Getting Started," "Launching," "Focus," and the "Hook."

A well-planned lesson approach will accomplish several important functions. First, it will prepare learners' hearts and minds for the Bible lesson by focusing their attention on the main idea of the lesson and establishing the importance of the lesson to their lives. For example, open a lesson on Christian suffering by asking participants to form small groups and to react (agree or disagree) with a statement, such as "a committed disciple of Jesus is always joyful." Second, the lesson approach will loosen up the class atmosphere and encourage continued involvement throughout the remainder of the lesson. Finally, it will allow time for the adult community building activities described in the previous chapter to take place. Remember, adult community building and Bible study activities can and should make mutual contributions to each other. Design the lesson approach to continue the community building process, while at the same time integrating with the lesson aims and leading into the focus of the Bible study.

The Lesson Development: Bible Study

In this part of the lesson, adults are led into a closer examination of God's Word. While some classes will primarily build their lessons around direct Bible study, other classes will choose to study extrabiblical topics that have practical value to the members of the class, in light of biblical truths. Whatever the format, the goal is for learners to discover what the Bible has to say in a specific chapter, book, section, or about a certain topic. At this stage, learners are seeking to understand more deeply the content and the meaning of the message the inspired biblical writers intended to communicate to their audience.

There are a variety of ways that adults can learn biblical truth. As emphasized throughout this book, adults respond best to Bible study methods that involve them in the learning process, allowing them to personally interact with the lesson truths and with each other. These methods may include group or individual research into Bible passages, creative projects, presentations, small and large group discussions, role plays, and a variety of other Bible learning activities. Adults especially appreciate those Bible study methods that focus on the practical points of the passage and those that have some kind of "hands on" participation. A combination case study and Bible search activity would be effective. For example, a teacher might give the class a typical case study that is related to the truths of the passage. The class would be instructed to search the passage to identify all of the principles that a counselor could use in an attempt to help the person in the case.

One adult class used a Bible paraphrase activity. The class was divided into pairs of students. Each pair was assigned a particular verse out of the lesson passage. The pairs were given time to write a contemporary paraphrase of the verse and read it aloud. The paraphrasing forced the class to grapple with the meaning and context of each verse. There are many possible options like the above. The adult learning information in chapters two and eight should guide you in knowing the appropriate methods to use with adult learners.

Bible study activities that make use of participant interaction also help with building adult community. As class members actively participate together in the process of studying God's Word, their hearts are welded together as a community. In essence, building adult community will take place throughout the entire lesson.

Although interactive methods are usually preferable when working with adults, several factors, such as the teaching topic, the learners' backgrounds and comfort levels, and the established learning culture will dictate how much and what kinds of interaction are appropriate during the actual Bible lesson itself. For example, when you have a very large class and the content is extensive or unfamiliar, a lecture may be necessary. You may liven up the lecture with some interaction, such as breaking the class up into "buzz groups" (see chapter eight). Attention to the established learning culture is also important. Even the best-developed interactive lesson plan would fail in a class comprised of adults expecting a Bible expository presentation. The wise teacher will seek ways to incorporate interaction slowly, by providing smaller interaction opportunities along with the biblical presentation. This may include worksheets, note-taking, fun quizzes, and questions and answers.

The Lesson Application

In all types of Bible studies, the ultimate goal is for the class members to learn biblical truths in such a way as to lead to a positive transformation in their lives. The discovery of biblical truth in the Bible study section of the lesson should never end there without a challenge for the learners to examine the biblical truth in light of their own lives.

For example, in the final several minutes of a lesson on 1 John 3 (which deals with expressing love), an adult teacher asked her class to name some kinds of people who need expressions of our love. The adults mentioned those who are ill, lonely, poor, depressed, and out of fellowship with God. After some discussion of these people, their needs, and how they can be helped, each class member was challenged to think of someone in one of these categories whom he or she could help during the following week.

This process of application involves two steps. First, learners are led to see possible ways in which they can apply the truths of the lesson to their lives. Second, they are encouraged to make specific plans to put this application personally into practice as soon as possible. Some curriculum publishers will make these two steps separate but related parts of the lesson plan. For example, Richards calls these two steps the "Look" and the "Took."[1] Other publishers will make them two phases of one part of the lesson.

Plansheets: The Session Organizer

Teachers sometimes find it difficult to keep all of the planned parts of the lesson straight in their minds. Even when they do, they may have difficulty with time management during the lesson. For example, the later the application activity comes in the lesson plan, the greater the possibility that earlier activities will rob it of its allotted time.

Be encouraged; a lesson plansheet can help! A planning guide can be used to assist the teacher (or teachers) step-by-step through the lesson development process. Teachers may want to put additional, more detailed lesson notes on separate sheets of paper. The plansheet, however, is the basic game plan for the entire Bible study.

Follow these steps to create a plansheet for teaching an adult class or Bible study:

1. Understand the Bible passage – The first step in teaching the Bible is to understand it as the first hearers and readers understood it. For this, you may want to consult various Bible translations, commentaries, and Bible dictionaries. Then you must understand what it means to us today and how it applies to our lives. While there are many applications of Scripture, there is only one meaning.

2. Identify the basic life-related principle – Summarizing the basic point of the passage will allow you to focus the direction of the lesson. This is sometimes called the "big idea."

3. State at least three lesson goals for your learners based on the basic life-related principle – You should select a cognitive aim (what the learners should know), an attitude aim (what internal perspectives, feelings, convictions, or values you want learners to gain), and a behavior aim (what the learners should be able to do as a result of the lesson). These aims must be written from the learner's perspective, not the teacher's. Good aims are brief, clear, and specific. Each part of the lesson should then be focused on helping to achieve the lesson aims.

4. *Plan the lesson approach* – This begins with the pre-meeting activities and continues up to the point of transitioning into Bible study. This should capture attention, give a reason to learn, and lead into the study.

5. *Transitional statement* – Identifying how the lesson approach activities relate to the upcoming Bible study is significant. This can often be accomplished through a simple learning activity or a statement that stresses the big idea, or life-related principle, of the lesson and why it is important to the learner's lives.

6. *Plan the Bible study* – Bible study methods should be determined that best lead to learning and to the achievement of the lesson aims, as well as match the particular learner backgrounds and learning culture.

7. *Plan the lesson application* – A significant purpose of Bible study for adults is the life application. Careful planning is necessary to assure that the proper amount of time is devoted to this part of the lesson and that the learning activities selected will allow class members to personalize the life application.

Post-Lesson Review

As presented earlier in this chapter, the first question to ask in preparing to teach a Bible lesson to adults is: "What do my class members need to get out of this?" After teaching the lesson, a similar question must be asked: "What *did* my class members get out of this?" This question answers whether purposes were achieved.

Plansheets can be used after the lesson and before the next lesson for evaluation. In the case of team teaching, each phase of the lesson plan should be discussed and evaluated. Places where time went over should be noted, as well. Teachers who teach alone should think through each part of the lesson in retrospect. It is a good practice to occasionally invite a spouse or other teachers or class members to help evaluate specific class sessions. Experienced teachers usually know right after the lesson is taught about its strengths and weaknesses. Ultimately, though, adult class or Bible study time is not evaluated according to what a teacher thinks or even how the participants felt. It is determined by the degree to which the lesson aims have been achieved. Once again, review the lesson aims you have identified for the lesson. Were they accomplished? How will you know? Teachers use many methods to assess whether their aims were achieved. Student projects, observations of student behavior and speech, student writing assignments, conversations with students, and written tests are just some ways to assess student learning. If your lesson aims have not been achieved, seek to understand the reasons for this. These reasons then guide future lesson preparation.

Summary

The goal of teaching adults is to help them learn. In preparing to teach a lesson, two questions must be answered: "What do my class members need to get out of this?" and "What is the best way for them to accomplish that?"

Plansheets are a great help in preparing to teach an adult class or Bible study. After you discover student needs and study relevant Bible passages or topics thoroughly, you must identify the lesson aims. There are three parts to a Bible lesson: Lesson Approach, Bible Study, and Lesson Application. Each of these sections should build upon the other and should lead to the accomplishment of the lesson aims.

Finally, after the teaching session, teachers need to evaluate the extent to which the lesson purposes have been achieved and then make adjustments in future lessons. Those purposes that have not been achieved can be incorporated into future lessons as learning needs.

For Further Discussion

1. How does a teacher enable adults to be self-learners?
2. Why are both a lesson approach and a lesson application necessary in Bible teaching? How can you ensure they are included?
3. How would you carry out an evaluation of the last lesson in which you participated? Did it achieve its purposes? In what ways? How can the results of the evaluation impact future lesson planning?

Notes

1. Lawrence O. Richards and Gary J. Bredfeldt, *Creative Bible Teaching* (Chicago: Moody Press, 1998), 168-174.

Choosing Adult Curriculum

~ 7 ~

Maybe more than once you have felt the frustration of trying to select just the right published curriculum for your adult class or study group. The choices seem endless! There are Bible book studies and topical studies. There are series that last for a whole quarter and those that last for only a few weeks. Your head is almost spinning with all the different publishers and their wide assortment of formats, "looks," and special features. How is an adult teacher to navigate the maze of selecting appropriate curriculum for his or her adult students? Whether you plan on writing your own lessons or using a published curriculum, all teachers must be informed about the curriculum selection process.

Identifying the Needs of Students

Perhaps the primary and most important step of selecting an adult curriculum is identifying the needs of your class participants. This is why many adult groups and classes often decide together what to study or what curriculum to choose. The last chapter discussed a few practical ways a teacher can determine the "felt needs" of learners. This section will focus in depth on developmental needs and local needs.

Developmental Needs
Cultural Life Stage Needs

For several decades educational psychologists have pinpointed with uncanny accuracy the developmental stages children undergo as they mature toward adulthood. It was not until 1978 that a similar sequence of adult life stages was also identified.[1] These studies on adulthood all speak with a united voice: "Adults generally face similar needs at similar stages in their lives." Bible teachers of adults would do well to listen to what they tell us.

However, it is important to remember that these are entitled *cultural* life stage needs for a reason. Although some developmental tasks listed below occur across cultures, many are based on contemporary American society's definitions of adulthood. These tasks may look differently or not occur at all, depending on a person's cultural environment, gender, race, or socioeconomic status. Even so, these developmental lists are a helpful start. The ETA course entitled *Understanding People*[2] offers the following outline of the various adult stages, with the accompanying tasks (related to physical, mental, socioemotional, and spiritual or moral development) that commonly challenge adults at each stage.

Late Adolescence (ages 18-22)
- Transition from being dependent to being independent
- Choosing a career or choosing a life partner
- Prime of life physically and sexually
- Mentally able to quickly and efficiently process large amounts of new information
- Ability to see many different perspectives on an issue (dialectical thinking)
- Forming meaningful and nurturing relationships (with friends and/ or life partner)
- Examining faith to make it one's own

Early Adult (ages 22-40)
- Peak body performance in early part of stage; first signs of aging in later part
- Primary reproductive years
- Diminishing youthful idealism in the face of realities and responsibilities of adult life
- Priorities: work, friends, family, independence (in descending order)
- Applying abstract and theoretical reasoning to life experience
- Strong critical thinking and decision-making skills
- Dealing with relational intimacy versus isolation
- Continued examination of faith to decide on beliefs and life conduct

☞ Moral development may reach higher levels, based on internalized principles

Middle Adult (ages 40-65)
☞ Many experience an overall sense of well-being and productivity
☞ Can be a time for reflection and reassessment
☞ Slight declines in hearing and vision
☞ Health concerns (heart disease, cancer, weight, menopausal risks)
☞ Family is priority; focus on giving back by investing in the coming generation
☞ Cognitive ability is strong, with a shift from *fluid* intelligence (short term memory, abstract thinking, and high-speed processing) to *crystallized* intelligence (accumulation of education and experience)
☞ Developing expertise in self-chosen areas allows creativity and flexibility for leadership
☞ "Generation in the middle:" caring for adult children and also aging parents
☞ Faith is on the verge of significant growth or prolonged stagnation

Senior Adult (ages 65 and beyond)
☞ Many are intellectually sharp, socially active, and physically able
☞ Increased physical challenges and diseases for some make health concerns a priority
☞ Vision and hearing loss heightens
☞ Slowing of fluid intelligence, with crystallized intelligence remaining steady (see above)
☞ Striving to reach the ultimate goal of wisdom, spiritual tranquility, and an acceptance of their overall lives
☞ Choosing passivity versus meaningful service and investment of wisdom in others
☞ Dealing with loss, depression, and acceptance of death as part of the life cycle

Only a very brief overview of these life stages and needs is presented here. The wise and caring teacher of adults will want to pursue further study of these life needs, especially the era of adulthood to which his class members belong.

Life Events and Transitions

Many developmentalists prefer to think of adult development in terms of life events and transitions. Life events are the significant happenings that shape and direct people's lives. These events are often seen as milestones that may or may not be tied to sequential patterns or specific ages. Some life events include graduation, marriage, childbirth, or the death of a loved one. Life events can also include events not occurring at the expected cultural life stage, such as infertility, singleness, and adult children living at home. Cultural events, such as a war, a natural catastrophe, or political movements also classify as life events.

Transitions (or life changes) mark processes that over time have the potential to generate personal growth and change. These can be triggered by life events such as a job loss or a prognosis of a terminal illness. Adults' lives are made of many transitions that can often be disorienting and require adjustment over time.

Significant learning can happen during times of discomfort and pain. As adults seek meaning in life's events, they may experience profound and fundamental changes in their worldview and values. Adult educators must seize these opportunities, offering their presence and support, while guiding adults into deep spiritual significance.

Local Needs

Every social unit experiences occasional or continual pressures that are felt by most of the members of that group and are unique to the local situation. Adult teachers need to be sensitive to the immediate common struggles of their class members. Though the class uses an ongoing curriculum program, the teacher should feel the freedom, and the responsibility, to temporarily set it aside to address pressing issues.

Group members are participants in at least two local communities: the community outside the church (the one in which they live and work) and the church community to which they belong. Occasionally the issues of each community may be of concern and addressing them in the adult Bible study group will be a wise ministry decision.

Issues Outside the Church

Each believer has many social responsibilities in his or her local community. Adult classes can help church members deal appropriately with these responsibilities. In communities in which corruption and scandals mark local politics, Christians need instruction concerning their biblical obligation to civil government. The decisions of local community leaders, businesses, and other organizations may occasionally oppose biblical moral values. Adult class members need to know how to respond properly. Religious cults infiltrate the community, requiring appropriate doctrinal armaments. The broader culture, media and technology, and world events also impact communities in specific ways. It is important to guide adults to relate to culture in a Christian way.

Issues Inside the Church

Some in-church factors that influence the curriculum of adult classes may be perpetual. For example, adult classes are wise to correlate with the pastor's preaching emphasis as much as possible, either by teaching similar topics or focusing on similar objectives.

Most issues within the church that affect curriculum planning in adult classes will arise more suddenly. A tragedy that has involved someone in the church or the class may call for a lesson, or even a series of lessons, on grief or the providence of God. The fall of a spiritual leader may cause a sense of disillusionment among the people. This, too, should be addressed from Scripture. An unusual slump in congregational giving may give occasion for a unit of lessons dealing with stewardship.

Selecting Curriculum Materials

After you discover student needs, consider the benefits to using a published curriculum versus writing your own. A published curriculum can be a time-saver, and it is especially helpful to inexperienced teachers; many writers of curriculum are experts in the field. However, published materials may not readily meet the needs of your specific class or group. Although writing your own curriculum often takes more time, it will allow you to cater lessons more directly to your unique students. Remember, even if you opt for a published curriculum program, you will still probably need to adapt the curriculum to your setting.

Once you decide to go with a published curriculum, you must face two sets of curriculum questions: (1) Will I primarily use topical studies or expository Bible studies? or (2) Will I follow an ongoing, long-range published curriculum program (such as a through-the-Bible series) or plan my curriculum one series at a time? Learner needs will help in answering the first question. Some classes find that alternating between topical and expository lessons is a good practice. This provides both an opportunity to study Scripture in depth and to focus on an application of the biblical studies to practical everyday issues. Depending on whether a church's pastor is primarily expository or topical in preaching style, the classes may want to emphasize a contrasting approach.

What about long-range versus short-range lesson planning? A professionally planned curriculum program offers the advantage of systematic and comprehensive Bible coverage. It also relieves teachers of the curriculum-planning burden. If used, teachers should not be enslaved to the plan. They should be sensitive to times when the plan should be adjusted to respond to the needs of the class. Many adult classes find that series-by-series curriculum planning provides more variety and a greater sense of expectation.

Curriculum Selection Pitfalls

The selection of curriculum materials is not easy. A good choice will take more than a Saturday morning visit to the local Christian bookstore. Adult Bible teachers are frequently misled by two common curriculum misconceptions: the generic curriculum fallacy and the fallacy of superficial selection.

The Generic Curriculum Fallacy

"Which adult Bible curriculum is best?" Christian education teachers and leaders face this question constantly. The correct question to ask is, "Which adult Bible curriculum is best for *my class*?" The key is to match the curriculum with the appropriate Bible class and teacher. And remember, there is no "perfect" or uniform curriculum. Teachers and students are the ones who really make a curriculum work.

The Superficial Selection Fallacy

All too often, curriculum selectors ask only these three questions when they look for teaching materials: (1) Is it attractive and colorful? (2) Is it quick and easy to use? (3) Is it inexpensive? Each of these questions has some value, but the problem with these three questions is that they all focus solely on surface matters. Curriculum selection based entirely on these superficial features probably will not meet the needs of the class. Frequent change from one curriculum publisher to another is an indication that curriculum choices are based on surface attractions.

Curriculum Selection Factors
Foundational Factors

The theological position, curriculum design, and educational philosophy of a curriculum are basic to everything in the curriculum. Because they are so important to good curriculum, every Bible teacher should know how to detect and evaluate them.

   1. Theology is the starting point. All Christian curriculum publishers design their materials to teach a certain doctrine to the adult learners, either explicitly or implicitly. Check the published doctrinal statement very carefully. Do you have any major disagreement with any of these doctrines? Is the theological coverage comprehensive enough for you?

   2. The curriculum design is the long-range plan used to systematize all the adult lessons in the total cycle that covers several weeks, months, or years. Publishers normally make it available with sample curriculum packets. Are you pleased with content coverage, sequence, and pacing?

   3. The educational philosophy of a curriculum program is related both to the publisher's theological position and the view of learning emphasized in its lesson materials. Educational philosophy is largely concerned with the way lessons deal with two major curriculum components—Bible content and student experience. Educational philosophy drives everything in a published curriculum.

Experiential
- ◆ Priority on experience
- ◆ Progressive
- ◆ Participant-centered
- ◆ Participants primarily active
- ◆ Discovery methodologies
- ◆ "Growth" metaphor

Biblically Interactive
- ◆ Priority on biblical content with design for optimum student interaction
- ◆ Transformational
- ◆ Teacher-led and student-involved
- ◆ Students active and passive
- ◆ Variety and balance in methodology
- ◆ "Travel" metaphor

Transmissive
- ◆ Priority on content
- ◆ Traditional
- ◆ Teacher-centered
- ◆ Class members primarily passive
- ◆ Telling methodology
- ◆ "Production/Factory" metaphor

Chart 1. Spectrum of Educational Philosophies

Chart 1 contains an overview of the two sides of the continuum of the major philosophies of curriculum in education, Experiential and Transmissive. Think of them as two positions on the path of a pendulum swing, with Experiential providing the opportunities for the facilitation of adult learning and Transmissive focusing on the traditional model of the teacher as the instructor and conveyor of content. In the curriculum selection process the teacher should consider the underlying educational philosophy. Which model is most compatible with his or her own educational philosophy? How will it be accepted by the class, considering the approach to learning that is most comfortable for them? Which model fits best with the principles of adult learning presented in this text? The Biblically Interactive curriculum model provides a balance between the Experiential and Transmissive curriculum styles, allowing for presentation of biblical content leading to the interaction of the adult group members.

Visible Factors

Visible factors of the curriculum are more apparent than the curriculum's theology, design, and educational philosophy. Although they may be more obvious, they are based upon the foundational factors just discussed.

The teacher's book is an important tool. It should be clearly organized into a step-by-step sequence of lesson procedures. Each lesson should have an aim or a set of objectives that gives direction to the lesson activities. These should emphasize the learning outcomes from the class members' perspective. What difference should the lesson make in their lives? There should be an appealing introduction that captivates attention and focuses on the theme of the lesson. The Bible study activities should lead the participants to learning the Word of God in an interesting way. Interpretation should be true to the context of each passage. Over a period of several weeks, a good variety of learning activities should be employed in the Bible study sessions. Each lesson should conclude with thought-provoking application activities that lead the student to apply the lesson truth for himself or herself.

Adequate teaching aids should be supplied with the teacher's material. Some of these may be in the form of suggestions within the teacher's manual. Ideally there also will be a separate teacher's resource kit containing a variety of teaching helps. Supplemental video tapes, CDs, DVDs, overhead transparencies, posters, charts, and student handout materials are the kinds of aids often provided by curriculum publishers. It is a mistake to think that creative teaching materials are only important for children's classes. They are enhancement for every age. Often, creative teaching materials are designed to help the teacher present lesson content. The contrast, however, should be true. All teaching materials should be used to increase participation and interaction in learning, not to subtract from it.

Participant books should be of high quality. Are they attractive, well-written, and stimulating? Will they make a valuable contribution to the success of class sessions? How will the participant materials be used? Will they increase participation in learning or subtract from it?

Implementing the Curriculum

Once the needs of the class have been identified and suitable curriculum materials have been chosen to meet those needs, another step remains. This is the most difficult step of all. How will the curriculum be used? The following guidelines for curriculum implementation will make the process more productive.

1. Do not hesitate to modify a published lesson plan to make it more meaningful for your class. Lesson modification may mean refocusing the emphasis of the lesson, substituting or supplementing the suggested teaching methods, or even dropping the lesson entirely. No one knows the needs of the class better than its teacher.

2. Limit the content to what is reasonable for class members to comprehend, remember, and apply to their lives during the given lesson period. Most published lessons never lack for content to be taught. Remember that Bible content is not the end—it is the means to the end. The desired end is transformed lives and the equipping of adults for service. All lesson content should be focused towards the application. Too much content detracts from accomplishing this goal.

3. Focus each lesson upon the response of the learners. Learners have an obligation to respond to God's truth. Teachers should be careful that they do not become so involved in the content of the lesson that they miss the opportunity to guide their class members into an appropriate response to God's Word.

4. Evaluate the impact of the curriculum on achieving adult learning objectives. The correct implementation of an educational curriculum is cyclical. After the curriculum has been implemented, it must then be evaluated—not on the basis of how the teachers and participants liked it, but on the basis of whether or not the goals of the class were met. If the goals were not met, then modify the curriculum (Step #1 above) or determine a new and different curriculum that will meet those needs.

Summary

Wading through the overabundance of curriculum options is never easy! The first step is identifying the needs of your adult participants, both developmental and local. Then, you will consider key questions related to the kind of study and the length of the study that is best for your class. Most importantly, you will consider the foundational factors of the curriculum. These factors will guide your decision about visible factors, such as the teacher's book, lesson plans, teaching aids, and participant books. Finally, as you use the curriculum, do not hesitate to modify or limit the plans for your class. Keep focused on the life response of your learners and evaluate the curriculum often in light of your goals.

For Further Discussion

1. List all of the relevant life stage needs for your adult group. Check the areas you have dealt with in your teaching over the past three years. What areas lack attention?
2. What are some of the life events and transitions your learners are facing? What curriculum topics may be appropriate?
3. Evaluate your curriculum materials in light of the information given in this chapter.
4. In your opinion, what are some key needs to be addressed in the adult Bible classes of your church?

Notes

1. Three prominent early researchers in adult development were Daniel J. Levinson, *The Seasons of a Man's Life* (New York: Ballatine Books, 1978); Gail Sheehy, *Passages: Predictable Crises of Adult Life* (New York: Bantam Books, 1974); and Charles M. Sell, an evangelical seminary professor and author, who wrote *Transitions Through Adult Life* (Grand Rapids: Zondervan, 1991).
2. Cheryl Fawcett, *Understanding People* (Wheaton, Ill.: Evangelical Training Association, 2000).

Methods for Teaching Adults

~ 8 ~

What does a teacher do with a class full of pragmatic, task-oriented, self-directed, and experiential adult learners? Although there is a time and place for using lecture and other presentation-based methods with adults, dynamic adult learning situations utilize group-centered and learner-centered methods. These methods invite greater participation from adults in their learning and allow more of the third "C" of Collaboration to take place. This chapter will help you to see how the adult learner characteristics of chapter two might look in a real classroom.

Guidelines for Selecting Methods

Methods are teaching activities designed to bring about specific kinds of learning. Your effectiveness as a teacher depends largely on your ability to use the right methods at the right time to achieve intended learning outcomes.[1] Here are some guidelines in choosing the most appropriate methods for an adult teaching situation:

1. Select methods that achieve your lesson aims.
2. Choose methods that are developmentally suitable to adults.
3. Use methods that you are adequately trained to use.
4. Select methods appropriate to your topic and setting (e.g., nature of the subject matter, group size, facility, learning culture, etc.)
5. Be sure all instructional materials and equipment are available.
6. Utilize a variety of methods that take into account your learner's learning styles, cultural background, interests, abilities, and so on.
7. Make sure the method fits the time available.

Teaching Tools

You should also consider the use of a variety of teaching tools that enhance learning. These tools may be printed tools (the Bible, books, worksheets), audio tools (music, CDs), or visual tools (objects, models, pictures, flipcharts, overhead transparencies, videos, PowerPoint slides).

With adults, using object lessons and visual or verbal illustrations from daily life can be effective. Jesus was a master at this technique. Think of how you might use your pet, your car, a TV program, or a trip to the grocery store to illustrate a lesson principle. Make use of a billboard on the way to work to drive home a biblical truth.

As much as possible, all of the five senses and multiple learning channels (auditory, visual, and tactile, or bodily movement) should be included in a lesson to meet diverse learner needs.

Categories of Methods For Adults

Interactive Methods

Since adults appreciate learning from each other, adult teachers should make use of methods that allow adults to interact with each other and share their collective experiences, expertise, and knowledge. As adults interact personally with each other and with the lesson content, they will understand the content better and apply it to their lives. They will also be challenged to accept other points of view and to correct or clarify their own thinking. These methods work best when participants are familiar with the content, when the task is clearly outlined, and when groups are monitored by the teacher.

Group discussion

Julie Gorman defines discussion as a "focused, orderly exchange of verbalized ideas, opinions, experiences and feelings in a collaborative setting."[2] Discussion requires a gifted facilitator able to guide the learning involvement of each class member. Discussions can take place as a large class (usually not larger than 20 to 25 students), in small groups, or in pairs. One of the main reasons discussions fail is poorly-worded questions. Good questions are:

1. *Open-ended* – A discussion leader's job is to draw out various points of view, to stimulate thought, and to invite personal reflection and response. Avoid questions with "yes" or "no" answers, either-or answers, or one-word answers. Stay away from leading questions, where one "correct" answer is sought.

2. Clear and concise – Avoid wordy or complex questions. If a question has two parts or there are questions within a question, be sure to ask only one question at a time to avoid confusion. Remember the more focused and specific the question is, the better.

3. Purposeful and relevant – The questions asked should be tied to the lesson goals. Adults will be much more willing to participate if they feel the questions are worthwhile, related to the topic at hand, and leading towards deeper learning that is important for their lives.

4. Inviting – The questions asked should be phrased in such a way that they are interesting and intriguing. They should also be welcoming and nonthreatening.

5. Scripture-based – Every question does not have to tie directly to a specific Bible passage, but questions should ultimately lead people to biblical truth. Sharing opinions and experiences does not necessarily change lives; the Holy Spirit does, through His Word. Conducting an *Inductive Bible Study* is one way to keep your group centered on the Bible. This approach invites participants to discover a specific biblical passage together: finding what it says, what it means, and how it generally applies to life. Specific, thought-provoking questions are asked to lead participants to observe, interpret, and apply a Bible text.[3]

Other Interactive Methods

1. Brainstorming – An adult teacher challenges the class members to quickly offer multiple ideas or responses related to a specific question or topic. All ideas are welcomed initially and recorded without evaluation. After many ideas are gathered, the class may select the most promising and relevant ideas to pursue further.

2. Buzz groups – This method is especially effective for promoting learner involvement after a presentation of information (such as a panel or lecture). A large group can be divided into smaller, timed discussion groups (from three to eight adults) with a particular focus. After the groups discuss their topic, a group representative may be asked to present their conclusions to the larger class so all can benefit.

3. Panel discussion – Two or more persons who have differing points of view on an issue, or who have expertise or experience in an area, are invited to speak to a class. The most successful panels are when the whole class is invited to interact with the presenters through the successful facilitation of a moderator. Invite some of your own qualified adult students to serve as panelists on a topic.

4. *Team teaching* – Invite your adult learners to join you in teaching, either temporarily or on a long-term basis. Enlist aspiring teachers into your lesson planning sessions. Switch leaders for discussion times. Allow adults to give interactive class presentations on various topics. Overall, create an environment of mutual teaching and learning.

Experiential Methods

Remember, your adults are focused on the real-life application in learning. They seek help in solving real problems or developing new life skills. Experiential methods feed this urge as they draw learners into direct, hands-on experiences that often involve the whole person in learning—mind, body, and heart. Your classroom can become more of a "laboratory" for living as learners are equipped to put the lesson truths into practice.

1. *Case studies* – Stories of how the truth of the lesson was applied or ignored by other people, help adults to see what it means for them. In a case study, a real or hypothetical problem or moral dilemma is presented for the class to analyze and resolve. Discussion should draw out many possible biblical solutions to the problem. To be most effective, these case studies need to be realistic and complex, with no clear-cut answers.

2. *Role play* – This involves class members acting out impromptu scenarios as a particular character. Role playing allows adults to identify with others and to try different approaches to a problem in a non-threatening environment. This method works best with adults when the focus is on situations they are likely to cope with today or tomorrow. Other forms of drama, such as short skits or scripted plays, can emphasize the life application of a biblical principle.

3. *Simulation* – These are games or activities that mimic reality. They are helpful when a real-life experience would be too impractical, dangerous, or expensive. Right in your classroom, learners can participate on a mock church elder board, build a team for an imaginary mission trip, experience a temporary "physical disability," or sit with the disciples at a recreated Passover dinner. The more realistic these simulations are, the better.

4. *Active Demonstrations* – This method is useful in practical skill training. A teacher or a class member first shows visually how an activity is done, and then others practice doing it themselves. This may be helpful when training adults to do one-on-one evangelism or to research a Bible passage online.

5. Modeling – Adults who are looking for help in practical Christian living will often imitate the actions of other adults who are spiritually mature. Jesus and Paul are the best examples of teaching adults through lifestyle example. As a teacher, you can involve your learners in relational experiences that allow them to watch and learn from other Christian adults. Reading biographies of great Christians is a way for learners to experience indirect modeling.

6. Field Trips – Sometimes it is necessary to take adults out of the usual learning environment to allow them to experience a different place or situation or gain a hands-on experience. For example, you may take a group of new teachers to visit another class or ministry to watch a master teacher. When you are discussing cultural differences, you may take adults to a neighborhood or restaurant of a different ethnicity.

Self-directed Methods

Adults appreciate the freedom to personalize their learning and achieve specific goals. As a teacher, you can offer learner-centered methods that increase learner choice and initiative. These methods will allow adults to express creativity and make individualized applications, and they are diverse enough to accommodate the needs of many types of learners.

A teacher must be sensitive to learners' needs and comfort levels. Since adults possess different levels of self-directedness, D. D. Pratt advises teachers to consider the learners' abilities and commitment when choosing between a more instructor-directed or learner-directed approach. Some learners who know very little about a specific content or a skill and lack either the commitment or the confidence to learn it on their own will probably need more direction and support from a teacher.[4] Other adults will be ready and able to design their own learning.

1. Learning centers – This involves designating a part of the teaching environment to a particular subject or activity. Learning centers are usually designed around a theme, and the most effective ones must be multimedia and at some level allow for learner selection and interaction.[5] Although these are mostly used with children, they can also be effective for adults, with age-appropriate adaptations.

2. Projects – Research has shown that adults participate in hundreds of individual learning projects every year. Allen Tough defined adult learning projects as organized projects with specific learning goals and a structured plan for achieving those goals.[6] Teachers can make use of practical, lesson-related learner projects as in-class activities or as applications that take place out of class. Research and reports, creative class presentations, surveys and interviews, construction projects, or other service projects are possible ideas. A personal Bible-memory plan or spiritual growth plan can also be an option. To inspire accountability, ask learners to create a project plan, listing the purpose, goals, activities, and date of completion. These plans can be signed agreements with a teacher or a peer.

3. Creative writing – There are many ways to use creative writing in teaching. For example, class small groups can write a make-believe entry for the journal of Lazarus on the day after his resurrection. Adult learners can also write prayers, Scripture paraphrases, short stories, poetry, imaginary letters, and plays in response to a lesson or to illustrate biblical truths being taught in class.

4. Creative art activities – Drawing, painting, sculpting, cartooning, or writing and performing music or drama can be used to reinforce a biblical truth. Dance or mime (acting with gestures only) are other possibilities. Some adults may find expression in photography, advanced audio or video technologies, and progressive computer programming and applications.

Critical Thinking Methods

Teachers must help adults to become critical thinkers. Adults must take time to reflect on what they believe and why. Ultimately, adults must be challenged to align all their thinking patterns with God's truth about themselves, others, their faith, and the world around them.

Dr. Richard Paul and Dr. Linda Elder of the Foundation for Critical Thinking describe critical thinkers as those who question information, conclusions, and points of view. These thinkers go beneath the surface and strive to be clear, accurate, precise, relevant, reasoned, and fair.[7]

Helping adults to be critical, biblical thinkers should be a part of everything you do, but here are a few specific methods that intentionally seek to engage learners in deeper levels of thinking.

1. Socratic Method – Rather than answering a direct question, the teacher will often throw that same question or another one back to the one who asked it, requiring the person to think about the issue. Jesus often did this (Mt. 9:14–17; Lk. 18:18–23). A key strategy is to continually ask others to clarify and support their statements or ideas. Other times, a teacher may challenge them with alternate or conflicting possibilities, playing a sort of "devil's advocate."

2. *Debate* – Opposing sides, composed of individuals or teams, can compete to try to persuade others of the validity of their point of view. To be effective, the proposition of a debate should be stated in positive terms, should be genuinely controversial, and should have research available on both sides.[8] Debate is effective in helping learners to analyze other perspectives, as well as develop research and communication skills.

3. *Pointed questions* – Paul and Elder list questions that can be asked at any time in the teaching process to probe learner thinking and hold learners accountable for their own thoughts.

- Clarity questions: Could you elaborate further on that point? Could you give me an example?
- Accuracy questions: Is that really true? How could we check that?
- Precision questions: Could you be more specific? Could you give more details?
- Relevance questions: How is that connected to the question? How does that bear on the issue at hand?
- Depth questions: What are some of the complexities of this question? What are difficulties to address?
- Breadth questions: Do we need to consider another point of view? Are there other ways to see this?
- Logic questions: Does this really make sense? Does that follow? Is there a contradiction?[9]

Informal Methods

Keep in mind that, for adults, much learning (some educators even argue, *most* learning) takes place outside the classroom. Adults participate in informal learning many times a day. Informal learning is the unexpected, spontaneous learning that occurs most often in a learner's natural setting.

As a teacher, one of your most important methods is your *presence*. As you spend time with adults inside and outside of class you can take advantage of "teachable moments." Casual conversations become opportunities to mention biblical truth. Questions raised may cause you to point adults to relevant resources. Challenging life events and transitions are opportunities for you or others to counsel adults into deep learning. Be prepared to use *all* of your interactions with adults as occasions for learning!

Summary

This chapter has offered possibilities to expand your "teacher's toolbox" of methods. Whether you choose interactive, experiential, self-directed, critical thinking, or informal methods, experiment to find which methods are most appropriate for your adult learners and goals. Do not be afraid to try a new method! If possible, research or receive training on the new method and practice it first in a neutral setting. The key is to use a variety of methods and tools to reach a variety of learners. Your adults will appreciate you as you teach them in the ways they learn best. Not to mention, they will be learning as well.

For Further Discussion

1. What teaching methods do you use the most? Why?
2. List as many methods and tools as you can that were used by Jesus.
3. What fears do you have in trying new methods? What are the benefits of using new methods?
4. Which new methods do you think your adult learners would benefit from? Discuss how to include them in your next lesson.
5. Using Jonah 1, plan an adult lesson using different methods.

Notes

1. For more extensive treatments of methodology see Kenneth O. Gangel, *24 Ways to Improve Your* Teaching; Jonathan N. Thigpen, ed., *Teaching* Techniques; and Marlene D. LeFever, *Creative Teaching Methods* (all listed in the bibliography).
2. Julie Gorman, "Group Discussion," in *Teaching Techniques,* ed. Jonathan N. Thigpen (Wheaton, Ill.: Evangelical Training Association, 2001), 66.
3. See the ETA *Instructor's Guide* for this course for more information on designing an inductive Bible study.
4. D. D. Pratt, "Andragogy as a Relational Contsruct," *Adult Education Quarterly* 38, no. 3 (1988): 160-181.
5. Jonathan N. Thigpen, "Learning Centers," in *Teaching Techniques,* 80-81.
6. Allen Tough, *The Adult's Learning Projects: A Fresh Approach to Theory and Practice in Adult Learning* (Toronto: Ontario Institute for Studies in Education, 1971).
7. Dr. Richard Paul and Dr. Linda Elder, *The Miniature Guide to Critical Thinking Concepts & Tools* (n.p.: The Foundation for Critical Thinking, 2001). See their website at *www.criticalthinking.org.*
8. Jonathan Thigpen, "A Taxonomy of Educational Methodology," in *Teaching Techniques,* 36.
9. Paul and Elder, *The Miniature Guide,* p. 7-8.

Creating an Adult Learning Environment

~ *9* ~

Everyone loved Eva's class. She always made the members of her class feel welcome. In fact, they would often try to get to class early to enjoy the relaxed atmosphere and the opportunity to be in comfortable surroundings with friends. Everything was arranged in the room to make each person feel comfortable. And, of course, the biggest thing was Eva. She had her own special way of making everyone feel at home.

When Eva was a member of Jerry's Bible study, she noticed he made a point of making everyone feel welcome and comfortable. It seemed so natural and easy since the Bible study met at Jerry's home, and his home was always a relaxing place for people to enjoy. The Bible study went really well, too. Group members were comfortable and relaxed as they discussed the Bible study freely and asked questions. After all, when people are thinking, they are more likely to be learning.

When Eva began teaching in the church, she thought about Jerry's Bible study at his home. She wondered why the same comfortable feeling could not be duplicated in a classroom at the church. She thought about what Jerry did to make everyone feel at home, and she did the same thing in the classroom. And it worked! Everyone felt comfortable in Eva's class and the environment made learning occur and personal and spiritual growth flourish.

The Physical Environment for Adult Learning

What would your dream classroom consist of for your adult class? A number of features characterize an adult classroom designed for maximum educational impact. Think of your adult classroom as you read the following pages.

Room Size

The size of the classroom should take into account the maximum attendance number the class is likely to reach. Recommended square footage per adult varies from twelve square feet to eighteen square feet. The amount of space needed depends on the teaching style of the class. Twelve square feet per adult make the classroom flexible enough for small group activities within the larger group. Eighteen square feet is recommended for innovative, activity-oriented classes. Since effective adult classes involve class members in active interaction with lesson truths and promote community growth, it is crucial that the size of the room provide the flexibility for adult interaction. If space is a problem, consider exchanging rooms with another class or moving to a larger room or a covered outdoor area for more interactive parts of the lesson.

Classroom Configuration

Classroom shape or width to length proportion is also an important factor. Square rooms are best for adult classes that are smaller and utilize general group discussions, but rectangular classrooms are best for larger classes that utilize small group activities. A 3:4 or 4:5 (width to length) proportional ratio is recommended for rectangular shaped classrooms.

Classroom Sound

Classroom sound should carry throughout the room. Class members in the most distant areas of the room should be able to hear the teacher and other class member's comments without having to strain to do so.

The sound should be soft, not reverberating harshly. Acoustical tile, carpeted floors, and drapes all help to combat the dreaded echo. The presence of class members will absorb some sound. Evaluate the acoustics of the room when it is full, not empty.

Classes placed next to noisy hallways, streets, air-conditioning or heating units, or other classes that regularly participate in loud activities are in for heavy competition. Take precautionary and reactionary measures when necessary to minimize noise distractions. Since adult classes rely on every class member sharing his or her gifts and knowledge with the rest of the class, it is crucial that everyone in the room is able to hear every other participant when he or she speaks.

Lighting

Classroom lighting demands will vary based on the activities planned; however, it is especially important to attend to appropriate lighting for class members to actively participate through reading, writing, and hands-on projects. A light-level meter can be used to gauge the quantity of light available.

Attention should be given to outside, natural light as well. Sunlight reflections or glares may sometimes be a distraction to learning. Be sure the room has adequate blinds to minimize unwanted sunlight, and check to see the room can be darkened for video or slide presentations.

Classroom Decor

The appearance of the walls, ceiling, and floor are the dominant decor features. Walls should be painted in pleasing colors or covered with attractive wallpaper or light-colored paneling. Overall, they should suggest a warm and inviting atmosphere. Consider personalizing the walls to reflect your class. Include pictures of group members or class events on bulletin boards. Feature a different group member each month, displaying their interests, accomplishments, favorite things, and family or cultural background. A message center near the door could be a place for class members to post notes, favorite cartoons, or prayer requests.

The most common deterrent to good decor is clutter. Eliminate outdated and unused furnishings. Store unused or irregularly used items neatly and possibly in another location. Take care to eliminate musty odors. You may have to open windows or use a room deodorizer.

Classroom Flexibility

Since adult classes use a variety of approaches to teaching, they will need classrooms that adapt to several different seating arrangements. Chairs, tables, and other furnishings should be able to move easily to achieve a variety of configurations. The seating arrangement should be designed to accommodate wheelchairs if necessary.

Adult classroom furniture need not be elaborate, but should be comfortable and attractive. For convenience and flexibility, tables and stackable chairs are best. Seating adults at tables accomplishes several things. Tables give students a place for coffee cups, a surface to write, and somewhere to place Bibles and purses. Tables automatically create a small group within a larger group.

If tables are not feasible, chairs should be arranged in a large circle or semi-circle so that all class members have an opportunity to see each other and the teacher during the class session. This also provides flexibility to move throughout the room for various class activities and to divide into small groups for discussions as needed.

The purpose of the room arrangement is to create an environment in which the group members feel comfortable. If the class has been meeting in rows, the sensitive teacher will allow them to continue in rows, introducing changes in seating gradually. On the other hand, a Bible study group, whose group culture is informal, will be most comfortable sitting in comfortable seats in a circle in a living room or family room atmosphere.

Marking Board or Chalkboard

Every teacher of adults needs ready access to a suitable marking board or chalkboard. Dry erasable marking boards, called white boards, are often more legible and certainly less messy. For most adult classes a 4 foot by 6 foot or 4 foot by 8 foot board is adequate.

Technology Equipment

A CD player, an overhead projector, and a videocassette/DVD player and monitor are all important. Many Bible teaching materials are available in these formats. Unless the adult classroom can be locked, it is probably best to store audiovisual equipment in a lockable room.

It is helpful as well to install a computer and an accompanying projector so that PowerPoint, DVD, the Internet, and other presentations may be used during the class sessions. Overhead projectors, and other kinds of projection equipment, are of little value without a suitable screen. You can use a portable tripod screen or one that is mounted permanently on the ceiling or wall. ETA's *TeacherTech* video will identify and tutor the novice through technical decisions.

Home Environments

The relaxed, informal setting of a home can be very conducive to adult Bible study or small groups. However, the drawback is you will often have less control over the physical setting. Keep the following points in mind as you plan for your group meetings.

1. Meet in a consistent and convenient location – Designate one home for meetings that is not too far in distance for most group members. If your group rotates among several homes, try rotating no more than once a month (assuming you meet weekly), and publish a schedule. This will help to avoid any confusion or a lack of attendance.

2. Find out about the home in advance – It is helpful to talk to the owners of the home first to find out more about the setting. If possible, visit the home to get a firsthand look. Be sure the home is large enough to accommodate your group needs (especially with seating) and has a room for meeting that will be relatively removed from outside distractions. Also, be sure the room lighting is adequate. Dim lights can lull group members to sleep or cause reading or writing problems. Room temperature should also be comfortable.

3. Try to minimize distractions in the home – Ask the host home to find a way to minimize phone calls or other family activities during the meeting time.

4. Set up in a circle or a U-shaped fashion – Be sure that eye contact is possible between everyone involved. Ask members to sit upright or even lean slightly forward, rather than sinking back into easy chairs or soft sofas.

5. Provide some form of refreshment – Food is always an added bonus to home group meetings! Homes are a natural environment for pre-session or post-session meals or light snacks. Members may take turns providing food for the group.

Facilitating an Adult Learning Climate

Effective teachers must consider the learning climate of teaching as well as the physical environment. The 3-C's of adult teaching—compassion, content, and collaboration—are the most significant resources for creating an inviting and positive learning climate. These three qualities must be integrated into everything the teacher does, every time he or she has contact with the group members. This includes before class, after class, during the class, and during the week. In a sense, the teacher's job never ends.

Pre-Session Learning Climate

Even before the session begins, the climate for learning is being created. Sometimes this even takes place in informal comments outside the classroom. As class members arrive, greet each one, making eye contact and shaking his or her hand as appropriate. Refer to concerns, events, or people in that person's life and help him or her feel comfortable. If a couple enters the room, be careful to greet each person separately and equally, helping them both to feel comfortable. If necessary, introduce a new person to others in the class, endeavoring to establish a connection by relating points of common interest they might share. Use this pre-session time to lead classmates into informal dialogue with each other, creating and maintaining class community.

This pre-session time is also a chance to begin your lesson approach. If you are using activity groups as part of your lesson approach, it is your task to integrate all new arrivers into one of the groups. These groups will create learning opportunities for everyone immediately upon his or her arrival, as well as allow group members to become better acquainted. Once everyone has arrived and the activities are taking place, the teacher needs to rotate from group to group, clarifying the activity and interacting with the members of each group. The teacher should be careful not to spend too much time talking with any individual group or group member and should allow the groups to complete the task independently. As soon as the group activities are completed, the teacher can bring the whole class back together for a time of reporting and discussion that leads into the upcoming lesson theme.

Facilitating Learning During The Session

Throughout the learning session, the teacher's persona, attitude, and approach to the class members can create the opportunity to learn in a positive, safe, and encouraging environment. A teacher who really cares about his or her class members will listen to what each member is saying, will try to help him or her to learn, and will value each person's contribution to the learning of the entire class. There are a number of ways you can do this.

Developing caring relationships – One of the best ways to encourage your adults to participate *in* class is to develop a relationship with them *outside* of class. Some adults may have special learning needs. For example, adults with various learning disabilities may need extra encouragement or time outside of class to review material with you one on one. Your care and compassion should be demonstrated in every contact you have with every adult class member. Then, as group discussions ensue, the members are anxious to participate because they know that the teacher cares what they think and appreciates insights they can contribute. As you demonstrate your care, others will be motivated to care for each other as well.

It is also important that you are open to sharing personal information about yourself in class sessions. This helps class members relate to you on a personal, genuine level. You may want to bring in photos of your family or other objects that display your interests and personality. At times, you may need to start off discussion by sharing your own feelings and struggles related to a lesson. Your openness and honesty will encourage others to share. Above all, feel free to be yourself. Use humor when appropriate. If the teacher is relaxed and confident, the group will be as well.

Eye Contact – Providing eye contact is why arranging chairs in a circle is so significant to an effective group discussion. Even when chairs are not arranged in a circle, however, eye contact with the participating class members is very important. "I think your contribution is important," "You are adding significantly to this class," or "Keep talking, you're doing a good job" are all messages that are communicated through good eye contact. Some teachers check their notes or write on the board or look at others in the room while someone is talking, but this actually discourages group participation. A lack of eye contact sends the message that what a person is saying is not important. This not only discourages that person from talking but creates hesitancy in others as well.

Affirmation – Everyone needs to be affirmed. This is even more important when some class members finally work up the nerve to participate in an adult group discussion. The more reticent the participant is, the more important the affirmation. Also, the larger the group, the more important the affirmation becomes.

Affirmation can be communicated in several ways. Again, eye contact is an important way. Many teachers make visual contact by moving closer to the person talking, nodding their heads in agreement, or making gestures with their hands or arms. Other teachers affirm participants verbally with comments such as "uh huh" or "good," and "thank you very much." Paraphrasing group members' comments and writing them on the board or flipchart is also an important way to reinforce what participants are contributing.

Although each teacher has a specific direction for the discussion, it is important for the teacher to have an open mind and be accepting of new or different ideas shared by the group participants. If the group members sense that the teacher is only looking for certain information or has predetermined what the "correct" answers are, they will soon lose any incentive for participating. They will also be hesitant to share if they feel that other group members will not accept their statements. Seek to create a safe, nonjudgmental atmosphere where alternate ideas are fairly and respectfully considered.

Guiding – The purpose of a group discussion is not just to allow an opportunity for group members to interact; it is also to achieve the learning objectives for the lesson. An effective facilitator will guide the discussion so that all the comments made by the participants contribute to the learning of the group. One way to do this is by writing class participants' comments on a board or flip chart. This not only affirms the contributions of the group members but it also guides the discussion, keeps the group focused on the lesson topic, and provides a summary of the contributions being made.

You will also want to keep the discussion moving by drawing out the key thoughts of the participants, related to the lesson. When there is a lull in the dialogue, ask questions like, "Would anyone else like to comment on this verse?" or "What else can we learn from this passage?" Your role is to continually guide the participants into deeper understandings of God's truth.

Your guiding of adults into learning will look differently depending on the group. Since the Holy Spirit is the teacher, it is impossible to prescribe a set discussion format. Sometimes, after asking a question, there may be complete silence. Silence is not necessarily negative. Adults may simply need time to ponder the question and formulate a response. In these cases, allow time to think, rephrasing the question for clarity. There may be other times, when the discussion moves away from the topic at hand. In this case, you may politely steer the group back to the original topic, suggesting the group pursue the unrelated topics at another time. If the unrelated topics seem worthwhile, you may want to allow them to unfold. Let the Holy Spirit and the class needs be your guide. Finally, there might be times when a group member will give an answer that is not in line with biblical truth. Remember, as a facilitator, your job is to ensure that in the end God's Word is clearly communicated. In a gentle way, you may want to ask the speaker to support his or her statement with Scripture. You may also ask for responses from other group members, allowing them to naturally correct the faulty thinking. A follow-up question to the speaker that invites deeper thinking may allow the speaker to correct the thinking on his or her own. Overall, the teacher must be sensitive to the

Holy Sprit's leading and guide the discussion according to the evolving needs of the class.

Maintaining Balance – A common challenge in facilitating adult group discussions is endeavoring to maintain a balance in the contributions of the various group members. Although it is generally not wise to call on specific group members, sometimes the quieter participants need some encouragement to share their ideas. Many facilitators, therefore, will call on group members who show non-verbal signs that they have a contribution to make (comments to neighbors, shifting in their seats, raising their hands, making facial expressions, or taking a breath as if preparing to speak).

Often certain members, or even sections of the room, participate too much. A gifted discussion facilitator will solve this in a number of ways, by either making eye contact with less vocal participants, asking those who have not spoken yet to respond, or limiting the response to only one side of the room. At times it may be necessary to talk to the more vocal participants privately, explaining the importance of balanced group participation.

This is one area in which small groups can make a great contribution. Often classes are either too large or are comprised of group members who are too talkative or too shy, making a large group discussion very difficult. By dividing the class into pairs or small groups and providing each group with a discussion topic, every person is able to participate. Also, by providing each group with a different topic, class members are able to interact with additional topics.

Summary

In the first five minutes a person enters an adult Bible classroom, he or she will determine whether it will be a positive experience or a negative one. This determination is made largely on the basis of the environment that exists in the room. The teacher and the feeling he or she portrays to the class members greatly influence this environment. If a relaxed, informal atmosphere is created, then the participants will feel more comfortable and able to focus on their own personal and spiritual growth.

The physical classroom is also a significant contributor to this positive learning environment through the configuration of the room, the arranging of the chairs and furniture, and the provision of the needed learning resources.

A key ingredient in helping adults learn is a gifted facilitator who will communicate a spirit of compassion and caring during the learning activities, using eye contact, verbal affirmation, and a guiding leadership style to use the equally balanced contributions of the group members to lead to learning.

For Further Discussion

1. What are the strengths and weaknesses of your physical classroom? What are the priority needs?

2. Specifically what can you do as a teacher to develop the most positive learning climate for your class?

3. What would you consider to be the key characteristics of an effective discussion facilitator? Compare your list to the principles suggested in this chapter.

4. Think of a discussion leader you have known. What principles did he or she follow? What principles evidenced needs for improvement?

Your Multicultural Class

~ 10 ~

When a Jewish leader asked Jesus, "Who is my neighbor?" it is fitting that Jesus answered with a story about a good Samaritan. In those days, there was much racial tension between Jews and Samaritans. Jesus knows the human nature well. He knows we often gravitate toward loving the "neighbors" that are just like us.

More and more, we must learn to love different neighbors. As increased mobility and technology bring our world closer together, men, women, and children of different ethnicities and cultures are finding the unexpected joys of learning to live and worship together. Ministries of the new millennium will each have to embrace diversity in their own ways. What can teachers of adults do to ensure that their teaching conforms to the Creator's vision of a great multitude from all nations, tribes, peoples, and tongues uniting together to worship the Lamb (Rev. 7:9)?

Embracing Difference:
A State of Heart and Mind

When studying diversity issues, we must first remember that every human being is an image-bearer of God (Gen. 1:27). Our many races reflect the multifaceted nature of God. Second, we must move away from the idea that difference is negative or wrong. Too often, we are quick to judge those who look or act differently from us. But God's Word says that difference is to be embraced. In God's family, every hand and every foot is needed and valued (1 Cor. 12). Christian unity happens in the midst of diversity! Our differences complement, challenge, and enable us to better carry out God's purposes.

At the heart of being a teacher is the desire to know, understand, and appreciate your students for who they are in all of their uniqueness and complexity. This involves a humble heart that says, "Maybe my way isn't the only way to do things," or "Maybe my perceptions aren't always accurate." There is flexibility here and a willingness to change. There is also an honest self-evaluation, which may at times involve repenting for any personal or corporate racism, even if it is subtle. You may need to reconcile with others or begin to show a new openness to learn from and embrace other cultural groups, as you welcome them into your life.

There are several practical steps you can take to know and appreciate your students.

1. Take an honest and informed look at your own cultural identity – Consider the ways it has shaped your values, beliefs, and practices. Step back to evaluate the strengths and weaknesses of your own culture and determine which traits are in line with biblical values, which are not, and which are not right or wrong, but merely culturally conditioned ways of thinking or behaving. Taking this time to reflect will help you to gain a new perspective on culture. As you see how your own culture has shaped you, you will begin to understand how it shapes others. You will be able to celebrate positive attributes of all cultures and join together with Christians from other cultures in pursuit of common biblical values.

2. Take time to learn the cultural background of every adult in your class or group – Begin a new class by asking everyone to share a little about themselves, including their cultural roots. Spend time talking with adult students, visiting their homes and communities and learning their individual and group histories. Relevant articles in your local newspaper, multicultural films or TV stations, and other books might give you valuable information about the cultures represented in your class. For example, you may want to locate a book about the African or Asian heritage reflected in the Scriptures. Rev. Walter Arthur McCray's book *The Black Presence in the Bible* and Dr. Cain Felder's book *Troubling Biblical Waters* are recommended resources on the African heritage.

3. Suspend judgment – When there is behavior that is baffling, do not label it negatively until consideration is given for any cultural meaning behind the behavior. For example, a teacher may perceive a student as inconsiderate for always showing up to class late. However, in some cultures, schedules are relaxed and relationships are valued over tasks; so fellowship along the way to class takes second place to punctuality. Remember that behavior is often a reflection of values. Seek to understand the cultural values of your group.

Multicultural Teaching and Learning

Multicultural teachers must begin to see their teaching methods, written curricular materials, lesson content, and the learning environment through new eyes! Part of loving your neighbor in tangible ways means carefully examining and evaluating every aspect of the teaching/learning situation in light of cultural differences.

It is beneficial to understand the general differences in cultural worldviews. James Anderson summarizes much of the writing and research on cultural differences into helpful categories.[1] Non-Western cultural groups (including most people of color and many Euro-American females) often emphasize group cooperation, harmony with others and nature, affective expression, and extended family. These groups more readily see the "big picture" (holistic thinking) and tend to have a flexible view of time. They are often more socially-oriented than task-oriented. Western groups, on the other hand (including some persons of color and Euro-Americans that are primarily male) emphasize individual competition, control of nature, limited affective expression, and nuclear family. They are task-oriented, tend to follow fixed time schedules, and more readily see distinct parts of a whole (dualistic thinking). Keep these diverse cultural frameworks in mind as you minister to your adult class, realizing that neither worldview is negative, just different.

Teaching Methods

Many theorists believe that each person has a unique learning or cognitive style that is influenced by his or her cultural background.[2] For example, some groups (usually non-Western) will appreciate gaining a sense of the "big picture" or the larger purposes of their learning. They may prefer to learn in relational settings where they can work in cooperative groups and discuss the lesson content with others (see Innovative learning style of chapter two). Since their learning is very connected to life, they will look for real life applications and experiences (see Common Sense learning style). Visual images are also very important to this group. Many non-Westerners think and communicate more in pictures and symbols, especially those that are concrete and drawn from everyday life.[3] Because of the emotion, humor, and life-based images found in stories, stories may be a way to engage this group in learning.

On the other hand, other cultural groups (often Western) may lean more towards an Analytic learning style. Those with this style prefer working on their own or with reference materials and often enjoy spending hours contemplating abstract ideas and theories. As "detail-people," they are skilled at tasks that involve working with specific, isolated facts and organizing them into ordered patterns.

Because learning styles may be different in various cultural groups, it is important to use diverse teaching methods. As this book emphasizes, balance the tasks of learning with the community-building aspect of the class. When lectures are necessary, offset them with discussions or group activities. When you are focusing on abstract Bible truths or theological concepts, make them more concrete with stories, experiential methods, and practical applications. Focus on broad themes or share summaries of the lesson at the beginning and end to show the total picture of the learning and why it is meaningful to learners. This will improve the learning experience for all.

Learning Environment

A positive learning environment (see chapter nine) is absolutely crucial in a multicultural classroom! The atmosphere should be personal, inviting and welcoming of difference. You should take an extra special measure to show care and affirmation, making sure that all adults feel safe and secure and included in class activities.

Part of creating a positive environment is helping learners to feel positively about themselves and others within the group. Many adults in your class may be wrestling with issues of cultural identity, especially those adults who feel tied to the cultural heritage of their ancestors, but also identify with another cultural group, usually the one they associate with from day to day. Others, who have experienced racial discrimination may feel a sense of low self-esteem. You can help adults to develop a positive racial identity by talking about some of these struggles in class times and by sharing relevant Scripture verses that speak of a Christian identity that transcends race, yet includes race as a beautiful creation of God. When discussing various points, seek to draw different perspectives from adults, asking them how their views have been positively influenced by their cultural heritage. Also, seek to find practical ways to celebrate cultural distinctness in class. One idea is to ask adults in your class to invite other adults over to share a dinner from their particular culture.

The teacher's role in a learning environment often looks different across cultures. In some cultures, the teacher is an unquestioned, authoritative figure that does most of the speaking. These cultures often have a high view of tradition and the past; their elders and authorities pass on revered content that has survived from generation to generation. In these settings, group cohesion and conformity are valued over personal autonomy and independence. Students in this tradition may feel threatened by debates or open challenge of a teacher or group member. Other cultures expect the teacher to allow mutual dialogue between the students and the teacher. Free expression, critical thinking, an exchange of varied views are expected and encouraged. As a teacher, you must be sensitive to these differences.

Discussion dynamics will also be important in a multicultural classroom. Although you want all students to participate, you should be aware of cultural ways of communicating. In some cultures, silence is viewed very positively, and reading nonverbal behavior or unsaid, subtle meanings is emphasized.[4] Because of this, students should never feel pressured to speak. At other times, adults will not participate because of a lack of understanding or confidence in the language used. In these cases, try to "read" nonverbal expressions or ask questions of non-native speakers to make sure they understand. Explain unfamiliar words and avoid cultural slang, using pictures and visuals often. Draw hesitant students into the discussion with less-threatening methods such as asking them to discuss a topic with the partner sitting next to them or to write an anonymous response on an index card that you will later read to the group.

Finally, it can be an eye-opening experience when you take a step back and evaluate your facilitation skills in light of cultural sensitivity. Do you make eye contact more frequently with those of your own culture? Do you respond more positively to comments or show more interest in comments from one cultural group over another? Do you subtly promote stereotypes? It may be helpful to have a trusted friend observe you in action.

Written Curriculum

The written curriculum can be a key factor in creating a positive multicultural experience in your adult class or group. Look closely at your teacher or student books, handouts, and instructional aids and examine them for cultural sensitivity. Ask several key questions: Are there diverse teaching and learning methods? Is the language understandable? Are there racial stereotypes? Does it challenge racial inequalities in society or merely reproduce the status quo? Is the content written from one dominant perspective? Is it relevant to the background and daily experience of those from different cultural groups? More than anything, adults want to be able to identify with the learning. They want to see role models that look like them. They want to see familiar people and familiar places, as they deal with issues that are important to them. This lets them know they belong and are valued members of the learning group.

Artwork in curriculum can be a silent, yet powerful communicator. If images of race are present, do they offer positive and accurate depictions of racial groups? Do the images depict multiple community settings? Do you see images from rich, middle-class, and poor classes represented? These are important issues to consider as you select a curriculum.

Power Dynamics

Finally, a teacher must be aware of power dynamics that exist in learning situations. Sadly, inequalities still exist in most societies today that can carry into the church if we are not careful. Talmadge C. Guy warns that "educational strategies, models, and practices that do not explicitly challenge the status quo only serve to reproduce it."[5] Through both speech and actions, the church must be a place that combats oppression and discrimination. It should model an alternative community of equity and justice and love of one's neighbor as a powerful witness to the watching world.

The adult class or group is the perfect place to start helping the voiceless in society to find a voice. First, adult teachers must see the wider community and societal context of their teaching. Many cultural groups are struggling to survive in an unsupportive, and even hostile society. They are fighting for basic needs such as food, clothing, shelter, and employment for themselves and their families. Their participation in church and educational opportunities is limited by these life-pressing demands. Adult groups must seek to meet some of these basic needs and consider how to change unsupportive societal structures.

Second, the third "C" of collaboration is especially important in these situations. Some adults may be hesitant to challenge the dominant voices in the room or to contribute their own ideas. You must intentionally invite all students to participate in learning activities. This collaborative effort instills a sense of value, equality, and power to all students. As you share power in the group, all can feel empowered and significant. As you involve all learners in curriculum decisions, you develop multicultural leadership that will impact a multicultural world.

Summary

Difference is positive! Our cultural differences reflect the creative design of our Maker. The start of creating a multicultural adult class is in our hearts and minds. We must gain a new attitude that seeks to know and appreciate our students in all their uniqueness. This involves examining our own cultural identity, learning the cultural background of our students, and suspending judgment. We must also take a look at the actual teaching and learning situation. A sensitive, thoughtful consideration of teaching methods, learning environment, written curriculum, and power dynamics is a beautiful demonstration of love for the neighbors that are right in our midst. Overall, you and the adults in your group will be transformed as you together uphold the vision of Revelation 7:9 in all you do.

For Further Discussion

1. What are some of the cultural differences in your class? How do these differences enrich learning?
2. Discuss several ways to welcome more diversity into your class.
3. What are ways your culture has shaped you? What are positives and negatives of your cultural group in light of biblical values?
4. What cultural worldviews are difficult for you to understand? What steps might you take to better understand and appreciate these different views?
5. Which aspects of your teaching situation (methods, environment, written curriculum, or power dynamics) need to change to better reflect multicultural differences? What can you do to change these?

Notes

1. James A. Anderson, "Cognitive Styles and Multicultural Populations," *Journal of Teacher Education* 39 (1988): 2-9.
2. See Ibid.
3. Anderson, "Cognitive Styles," 7.
4. Carol A. Jenkins and Dale Kratt, "Sociological Foundations of Multicultural Religious Education," in *Multicultural Religious Education*, ed. Barbara Wilkerson (Birmingham, Ala.: Religious Education Press, 1997) 56-92.
5. Talmadge C. Guy, ed. *Providing Culturally Relevant Adult Education: A Challenge for the Twenty-first Century*, New Directions for Adult and Continuing Education, no. 82 (San Francisco: Jossey-Bass, summer 1999), 94.

Gender, Generations, and Growing Groups

~ 11 ~

Who are the people that make up your adult class or group? Maybe you lead a women's Bible study or a men's small group. Maybe your class is made up of adults from the same generation. For example, you might be enjoying a class full of active senior adults, or trying to challenge a handful of young adults to examine God's Word. Possibly the singles ministry is expanding at your church and you have been asked to take on a Bible discussion group for singles. Or maybe your group is an eclectic mix of both men and women of multiple ages from various walks of life. Whatever your class combination, you will gain a better sense of gender and generational differences, and you will come face to face with three of today's growing adult groups, who often have untapped gifts and unmet needs: senior adults, singles, and persons with disabilities.

Gender Differences

The differences between the genders go back to the Garden of Eden. God has made us male and female and has declared it very good (Gen. 1:27). Each gender is valuable and necessary to the Body of Christ and contributes complementary strengths. Whether you teach groups of the same gender or mixed gender groups, you will find that gender is an important dynamic in adult learning.

First, keep in mind that men and women often enter your teaching situation with different motivations. In her book entitled *In a Different Voice*, researcher and author Carol Gilligan suggests that men find fulfillment primarily by achieving and separating themselves as individuals, while women find their identity primarily through attaching themselves to others and being interdependent in a network of relationships.[1] Because of this, men may seek out learning more for the challenge of learning new material, gaining a skill, or sharing their expertise with others; women, on the other hand, may be looking more to establish or maintain relationships and be part of a community where they can explore feelings, make connections, and share experiences.

Gender dynamics in same-gender groups look different than in mixed-gender groups. Longtime Christian educator Julie Gorman cites research from many studies, giving us general patterns and characteristics of men and women in groups.[2] She says that both genders appear to be more task-oriented in same-gender groups. All-male groups, however, tend to be more competitive than female groups and take longer to form a cohesive unit. Women generally prefer small groups of the same gender due to the high level of personal disclosure, while men show preference for mixed-gender groups of various sizes.

In mixed-gender groups, Gorman notes that gender distinctions are less pronounced as men and women adapt to each other and gain different perspectives. Men seem less competitive, more relationally aware, and more able to disclose personal information. Women, on the other hand, are less likely to take initiative or adopt a leadership role in mixed groups, even though they appear equally capable. They also tend to talk less, ask more questions than men, and use more language (such as verbal fillers, qualifiers, or disclaimers) that may convey a lack of conviction or confidence. The women who do speak with confidence may feel judged for being "too capable."[3] Men, in contrast, use more direct forms of language to influence others. The topics men introduce in a discussion are more likely to be explored by the group.

An awareness of group gender dynamics should guide your teaching. First, decide whether a same-gender or mixed group will best serve your goals. Same-gender groups may be preferred when your topic is sensitive or gender-specific. Second, it is important to encourage collaborative rather than competitive learning in all gender settings. This does not mean you cannot allow a healthy debate, but enclose it in a context of love and acceptance. Finally, in mixed-gender settings it is especially important to allow the two genders to hear and learn from each other. Invite all to speak equally, encouraging and affirming hesitant members especially. Allow both men and women to be involved in group decisions and to use their gifts to serve and lead others. Keep a balanced focus on the teaching task and the relational dynamics of the group, making sure to value experience, feelings, and intuition as ways of knowing and learning in the classroom.

Overall, seek to foster an environment that celebrates and learns from gender differences. In a culture that tries to minimize gender differences or pit one gender against the other, it is especially important that Christian adult groups reflect a biblical image of gender relationships. As you teach, help adults to develop a healthy gender identity by addressing gender issues from a biblical perspective.

Generational Differences

Each generation has something to teach the church. King David writes, "One generation shall praise Your works to another" (Ps. 145:4). Older generations are to tell the generation to come the "praises of the Lord" and "His wondrous works" (Ps. 78:4). Those from younger generations as well are instructed to set an example for the believers in "speech, conduct, love, faith and purity" (1 Tim. 4:12). Although many churches segregate the adult generations, there are many benefits to an intergenerational approach with adults.

A generation is a group of people growing up in a specific historical and cultural time period. Demographers often use different dates to define the various groups, so it is hard to say exactly when one generation begins or ends. However, it helps to speak of generational differences in terms of values. In their book entitled *Boomers, Xers, and Other Strangers*, Rick and Kathy Hicks say that the critical time for developing values that shape our adulthood is in our youth.[4] The historical events and cultural milieu of our formative years have a profound impact on us, and often those who grow up together (a generation) share the same values.

Hicks and Hicks help us to gain an understanding of the characteristics and values of different generational groupings in American society:

Builder Generation – Born between 1901 and 1945

Also called the Depression Generation, this group consists of two smaller groupings sharing the same basic values: the GI Generation (born 1901-1924) and the Silent Generation (born 1925-1945). The Builders, having survived one or both world wars, are known for their strengths at building and rebuilding society after crisis events. They espouse traditional family values, personal discipline, self-sacrifice, commitment to country, and saving money. They have a high work ethic, like to work in teams, and want to follow a task until completion.

Baby Boomers – Born between 1946 and 1964

Known for their sheer size in numbers, this generation has had impressive power to change the status quo. In their idealistic younger years, they challenged existing societal structures and rebelled against their parents' traditional moral values and religious beliefs. As they settled into careers, they focused on personal and financial fulfillment, at times to the neglect of their family. They value spending money over saving it. In recent years, many younger Boomers are returning to traditional values of Builders as they fight to protect their children and themselves from increasing social ills.

Generation X – Born between 1965 and 1983 (or 1965 and 1976)

Often called Baby Busters due to their relatively small size, this generation grew up in difficult financial and family times with many experiencing divorce. The abandonment they felt from societal institutions led some to be skeptical, cynical, and non-committal. The first generation to grow up with Postmodernism as the dominant perspective, they are morally relativistic and value tolerance, authenticity, personal experience, emotion, and practical living. Their work style preferences include independence, individuality, flexibility, and a balance between work and outside relationships. Recent research has shown a grassroots movement of serious and passionate young Christian adults from this generation with more conservative theological and moral beliefs than their Boomer parents and a renewed interest in traditional church practices – such as liturgy, creeds, and Christian classics.[5]

Millennials – Born between 1984 and 2002 (or 1977 and 1997)

Hicks and Hicks call this generation the Net Generation (or N-Gen). Others call them Generation Y or the Mosaics. Their identity is still taking shape as the oldest Millennials begin to emerge on the adult scene. Increasingly diverse racially, and larger in numbers than the Boomers, they are the first generation to grow up with access to the Internet. They are global-minded and technologically-savvy. They are upbeat and optimistic about the future, demonstrate positive self-image, and value education as a means to financial success. Members of this generation seem to respect and appreciate the influence of elders and parents more than Boomers or Xers. So far, their work style seems to emphasize teamwork, innovation, and multitasking. Their high participation levels in volunteer service and civic events have led some generational experts to compare them to the Builder generation.[6]

Intergenerational Teaching

An awareness of generational differences will impact your teaching. In a time of shifting moral values, Builders can be a structure of support helping younger generations to stand for truth and develop a consistent Christian worldview. The younger generations, on the other hand, can help the Builders to break out of tradition and try new things.

Understanding the generations will help you to resolve potential conflicts. Hicks and Hicks tell us the differences between generations are not merely age or styles of dress but "gut-level differences in values that involve a person's beliefs, emotions, and preferences."[7] Consider the potential generational value conflicts in financing a new church building, choosing a new pastor, welcoming racial diversity, choosing Sunday morning attire and worship style, or making innovations in church programs. In these situations, promote dialogue and understanding between the generations about underlying values.

Keep a balanced and varied teaching environment. Balance the teaching task with relationship-building. Builders want to follow a task until completion. Xers and Millennials often value the process over the product. They are focused on the relational and experiential aspect of learning, and often enjoy methods that touch their senses and emotions, such as stories, testimonies, drama and art, and experiential methods. All generations will benefit from interactive and varied methods. Also, keep a balance between Bible content and application. All generations will benefit by a focus on how the Bible works in real life and how they can serve others.

Be authentic in your manner and approach. Xers and Millennials value genuineness and substance over slick exteriors and credentials. While Boomers tend to prefer large gatherings where they can network with many acquaintances, Xers prefer smaller, more intimate gatherings with close friends. Also, look for ways to share leadership within the classroom. Boomers and Xers especially will be turned off if a teacher tries to act like the expert or the unquestioned authority figure. Promote an equal plane of relationships, where leadership is often shared and members are free to challenge and question held assumptions.

Growing Groups

Senior Adults

Senior adults (ages 65 and older) comprise the fastest growing segment of the North American population. Currently, there are nearly

67 million Americans over the age of fifty, and this number will only increase as the Boomer generation begins retiring en masse. Many seniors are satisfied with their lives and are intellectually sharp, socially active, and physically able for years longer than previously imagined. In fact, seniors volunteer more than any other age segment. Is the church ready to minister to and with this graying yet infinitely valuable senior adult population?

Pastor to senior adults Dr. David Gallagher gives us a profile of today's active senior adults.[8] He tells us they want to be with like-minded friends in a warm, loving, and caring church family and that they are willing to sacrifice for a worthwhile cause. They respond well to creative teaching, appreciate a caring pastor and staff, value stability and predictability, and like to show respect to authority and to their rich heritage. They can accept change, he says, but prefer gradual change that has a meaningful purpose. Additionally, seniors are known for their undying loyalty and their deep appreciation for institutions and organizations that have touched their lives. They want to be busy, to serve, to talk and to share their experiences and their faith in simple, relational ways. Many of them absolutely love to be around children, youth, and young adults.

For many senior adults, however, there are very real struggles. Some are homebound or in need of short- or long-term care. Others are dealing with loss, grief, disease, and even depression due to a sense of powerlessness or insignificance in their lives. Many are spending time reflecting over their lives and seeking to gain a sense of peace and satisfaction. The adult teacher can minister in caring and tangible ways to these seniors by promoting respect and appreciation of seniors within the church congregation. Seniors feel significant as they are invited to share their stories and years of wisdom with others.

Other ways to minister to needy seniors are numerous. Visiting shut-ins, helping with car repairs, delivering meals, and offering companionship are just a few ways you and your class can serve seniors. Seniors will experience self-worth and love when someone takes initiative to follow up with them, particularly if they are new to a church or class or have been absent. Use telephone calls, personal visits, and post cards to let them know that they are valued. When the church is loyal to the senior, the senior will be infinitely loyal to the church.[9]

For active senior class members, be sure to plan social gatherings and activities. Boat cruises, bowling, museum visits, concerts, lunches, ice cream socials, and billiards are just a few activities that seniors may enjoy. Early morning activities are also popular with seniors.

Within the classroom, seniors value innovations in teaching style as long as the structure is not constantly changing or shifting. Necessary changes need to be purposeful, gradual, prayerful, and discussed in advance. It is also important to be sensitive to the vision and hearing needs of your seniors in the classroom. Order large print Bibles when possible. When hearing loss is obvious, speak loudly, clearly, and slowly so that adults can read your lips or hear your words. Use a sound system for added volume.

Connecting loyal, active seniors to areas of service within the church fosters growth and community. Seniors can offer wisdom through serving on church boards or committees, tutoring, and helping in children's ministries. Often their homes make ideal places for housing visiting missionaries or church guests. Seniors are also frequent paricipants on short-term mission or service projects.

Singles

The population of single adults in America is exploding! Many young adults are putting off marriage for many reasons, such as finishing their education, pursuing careers or ministry, or wanting to find the "right one." Single adults vary in age and include those who are never-married, divorced, separated, or widowed. Each of these groups contains single parents. Unfortunately, singles often feel marginalized in a church that is centered on couples and families. In fact, those who are single and never-married are more likely than other groups to be unchurched.[10]

The main problem singles experience in the church is one of attitude. Many see singleness as a stigma, rather than the gift God has intended it to be (1 Cor. 7:7–8). We must begin to see singles with new eyes. Whether adults are single for a season or for life, it is a special time to be undivided in devotion to the Lord. As you accept the status of the single person, you will also help singles to accept themselves and the single season, viewing it as a time to develop personally, vocationally, relationally, and spiritually.

One way to effectively relate to singles is to provide them with a place to belong. Some are far from their families and lack deep relational roots. Allow your classroom to be a place of stability where they can know others and be known. Encourage older, spiritually mature people within your classroom to mentor younger single Christians.

Teaching on relevant topics will also help the single adult to feel connected and valued. Topics that often resonate with single people are self-worth, intimacy, dating, goal and career planning, finances, housing needs, car repair, sexuality, and stewardship. Singles of different ages will have different developmental needs to consider. In fact, they will probably have more in common with married adults of their age group than singles of another age group.

Provide healthy family models to single Christians by connecting them with families within the church. Singles do not always want to be with other singles! Singles are often blessed through family activities, such as home-cooked meals, playtime with kids, or family vacations. When families within the church open up their homes to the single population, they will find that they will not only bless and encourage the single person, but they will also be blessed and encouraged.

Encourage singles to become active members in the larger church congregation. Invite them to accompany you to church-wide events. Connect them to ministries in the church where their gifts can be used and appreciated.

For those people in your group who are previously married and now single, offer care and unconditional support. Welcome divorced or separated singles, who often feel negatively labeled by the church, into your fellowship. Some may find help in divorce recovery classes or remarriage counseling. Widowed singles may benefit from a grief support group. Singles with young children may appreciate help from others in the form of babysitting, car repair, finances, and meals. Church members can also serve as adult role models for their children.

Persons with Physical Disabilities

As of the 2000 United States Census, 18.6 percent of the adult population between the ages of 16 and 64 had some form of disability. That is almost one-fifth of the population! Today's adult teacher will inevitably have adults with varying degrees of disability in his or her classroom, which will present its own unique challenges and rewards. Entire books have been written on the different types of disabilities and how the teacher can effectively reach and minister to each one. This section will focus on physical disabilities, giving general suggestions for accommodating the needs of the physically challenged students in your classroom.

First, learn who, if anyone, in your classroom has a physical disability. Some disabilities may not be readily apparent. Whether someone is hard of hearing, visually impaired, or in a wheel chair, each individual will have specific needs. Once you learn who has special needs, learn as much as possible about the specific disability. Reference the Internet or library for material that will inform you of the characteristics and challenges of each disability as well as ways that you, the teacher, can be sensitive to various needs that coincide. Becoming informed is the first step in making the most of the educational experience for your students. A sensitive teacher who actively seeks to understand and assist in making education a pleasant experience will be much appreciated by the student.

Second, go to these students individually and ask if they have need of any assistance or special consideration. Their particular disability may not require any accommodation. On the other hand, they may be extremely grateful for the thought and may, indeed, have some suggestions. Visually impaired students may need a brighter environment or may need the writing on the blackboard or on printed documents to be larger. They may need to sit closer to the front of the classroom. Students in wheel chairs may need desks that better accommodate the space a wheel chair uses. Students with hearing difficulties may need an interpreter or may need to sit in a place where they can also read lips. Braille books or books on tape can be a blessing to some students. Each disability produces different needs. Seeking out those students and their particular needs allows for each to benefit from the classroom experience.

The key to being successful with challenged students is to be informed, sensitive, and active in helping them to get the most out of their learning experiences. This will allow the teacher to navigate through the needs of each and every student, ensuring that all are learning and growing.

Summary

No matter what group of adults you teach, gender and generation will always play a role. In mixed gender or intergenerational groups, you will experience the joy of complementary strengths. You also may experience conflicts or misunderstandings between the genders or generations, but these can be opportunities for mutual learning. Structure your teaching to meet different needs through collaboration, equal participation, experiential learning, multiple methods, practical application, and an equal focus on relationship and task. As you encounter senior adults, singles, and persons with disabilities in your teaching, let them show you how to minister to them as they minister to you as well. Above all, keep a humble heart and an open mind as you seek to know, love, and appreciate all your adult learners as God's unique and wonderful creations.

For Further Discussion

1. What gender dynamics have you observed in your adult class, whether it is a single gender or mixed group?
2. What generational conflicts have arisen in your church or ministry? How were these resolved?
3. What are the benefits of intergenerational groups?
4. List the different people in your adult class or group. What insights from the chapter will you use to better minister to them?
5. What growing adult group do you need to learn more about? How will you do this?

Notes

1. Carol Gilligan, *In a Different Voice* (Harvard: Harvard University Press, 1983).
2. Julie Gorman, *Community That Is Christian: A Handbook on Small Groups* (Wheaton, Ill.: Victor Books, 1993), 241-258.
3. Edie Schultze, "Gender Dynamics in the Classroom," *Wheaton* 3, no. 2 (spring 2000): 20-21.
4. Dr. Rick Hicks and Kathy Hicks, *Boomers, Xers, and Other Strangers* (Wheaton, Ill.: Tyndale, 1999).
5. See Colleen Carroll, *The New Faithful: Why Young Adults are Embracing Christian Orthodoxy* (Chicago: Loyola Press, 2002).
6. Neil Howe and William Strauss, *Millenials Rising: The Next Great Generation* (New York: Vintage Books, 2000).
7. Hicks and Hicks, *Boomers, Xers, and Other Strangers*, 4.
8. David P. Gallagher, *Senior Adult Ministry in the 21st Century* (Loveland, Colo.: Group, 2002), 13-29.
9. Ibid, 21.
10. Barna Research Group, "Number of Unchurched Adults Has Nearly Doubled Since 1991," *Barna Update*, 4 May 2004, <http://www.barna.org FlexPage.aspx?Page=BarnaUpdate&BarnaUpdateID=163> (17 August 2004).

Settings for Adult Learning

~ 12 ~

Learning is a never-ending process for the Christian! Adults in your classes and Bible study small groups should be continually seeking to mature and grow into all God wants them to be. Like Jesus, they will continue to develop mentally, socially, physically, and spiritually throughout their lives (Luke 2:52).

There are many settings where adults can experience growth. As a teacher, it is important for you to be aware of the various types of adult Christian education that are provided in your church or community so you can serve as a reference for your adult class or group and encourage adults' pursuit of lifelong learning. In all of your teaching endeavors, you will seek to create a dynamic and life-transforming learning experience for your adults by following the seven keys to effective adult learning, as expressed throughout this book.

Settings for Learning

Sunday School

Historically a ministry to children, the Sunday School has since broadened to include the entire family. Even so, the Sunday School ministry in most churches is still primarily viewed as a ministry to children. This has created a special challenge to those teaching and leading adult Sunday School classes.

A Sunday School ministry, however, can be very effective for adults. Adults are at the church already during that time, either attending the worship service or bringing their children to Sunday School classes. It is also a great opportunity to provide Bible learning for the adults in the church. Many churches offer elective classes on biblical topics or studies. Even in churches blessed with a gifted Bible expositor as a pastor, Bible learning in a structured class environment greatly enhances adults' ability to deeply learn God's Word and apply it to their lives.

Evening Bible School or Institute

Some growing churches have experimented with double services and double Sunday Schools, with the adults attending the worship service and the children attending Sunday School simultaneously. Then, either on Sunday evenings or possibly on another night of the week, classes are provided for adult learning. Often this can be a more formal Bible school for church members or a community-wide Bible institute with multiple classes offered during the evening. These classes can be geared towards all adults or specifically to lay leadership training for various aspects of ministry. Adult education credits and certificates can also be granted for student incentive.

Retreats and Seminars

Churches may sponsor several types of adult retreats—couple's retreats, family retreats, singles' retreats, leaders' retreats, and so on. These often mix learning with relaxation and recreation and may last for a day, a weekend, or longer. Campgrounds, hotels, or retreat centers are popular locations for retreats. Other churches offer adult seminars or workshops on various topics. These may be church-sponsored or part of a larger, independent conference. Many churches send their adult teachers and leaders to various denominational or other kinds of training conferences. To make these kinds of events most useful to adults, it is recommended they set specific personal goals before attending and discuss specific plans for application of learning with other attendees after the events are over.

Christian Colleges and Seminaries

Christian colleges and seminaries are providing more non-degree and degree programs geared especially for adults. Many schools offer courses that fit adults' busy lifestyles, such as evening classes, correspondence courses, online courses, weekend classes, and summer school sessions, and the fee structures are more appropriate to part-time, non-traditional students.

Bible Studies

Bible studies for adults are typically more informal in style than the school-oriented adult educational programs. These Bible studies may meet in churches, homes, schools, businesses, and other locations during weekdays or evenings or on weekends. The leaders or those hosting often serve refreshments and make an effort to provide a relaxed environment in which adults can encourage each other, develop closer relationships, and learn the Bible together.

Small Groups (in various settings)

Many churches divide their membership into smaller groups for fellowship, spiritual growth, and possible outreach efforts. These groups meet periodically, sometimes for social events, such as dinners, cookouts, and sporting events, and other times for times of prayer, discussion, and Bible study. Some of the groups make an effort to invite their unsaved neighbors and friends. Fellowship groups in people's homes provide a safe, non-threatening entrance for the unchurched into the larger church fellowship and allow adults the opportunity to learn and apply God's Word in a relaxed atmosphere. These small groups may also meet in restaurants, coffee shops, or rooms in the church.

Informal and Self-directed Learning

Churches can support adults in their independent learning pursuits, whether informal or self-directed learning. Some churches provide devotional guides, a list of Bible reading passages for the week related to the pastor's sermon, or a theme for the church community to study during specific months of the year. A church library or bookstore can also serve as a valuable resource for adult learning. Independent adult learning projects are often incorporated into a church's more formal educational programs, providing projects for adults to complete and then report back to the group. Sometimes, these learning projects can form the basis of a longer presentation or a church class in and of themselves.

Other churches may promote informal adult discussion groups. Teachers, leaders, and pastors can provide statements and questions to encourage people to think and to discuss. Statements can also be placed in the church bulletin, on the church bulletin board or the church sign outside that will capture the attention of the church membership. The topics for these discussions are endless! Some churches have adult groups that discuss the sermon each Sunday, discuss a special book (book discussion group or "book club"), or discuss special pertinent theological or biblical topics. Adult discussions can take place during the week in person, on the telephone, and through email. They also occur in the narthex, the hallways, the worship centers, and outside the church building on Sunday mornings.

The Internet

The Internet can be a wonderful tool for adult learning. Most colleges, even Christian colleges, now have courses available on the Internet. Churches can offer educational opportunities as well. Email lists, chat rooms, and discussion boards on church websites all provide excellent opportunities for adults to keep in contact during the week and to continue discussions that will help them learn and grow as believers in Christ. Church websites can also provide links to other sites or recommended resources that provide additional information for adults interested in pursuing research or participating in computer-based informal learning. The variety of learning opportunities for adults is limited only by our own creativity!

The Seven Keys To Effective Adult Learning

Adult learning does not just happen. It results from careful consideration and application of the time-tested keys to effective adult learning that have been discussed in this book. These keys involve the role of the teacher, the facilitator of learning. They also involve the environment for learning, the curriculum and goals, and the participation of the class members themselves.

Key #1—Vision for Teaching

Effective adult Bible teachers know why they do what they do. They are motivated by the goal of training adult leaders for the expansion of God's kingdom. Ultimately, they want to bring God glory in all they do. They follow Christ's command to teach adults as they support them in the areas of spiritual growth, biblical literacy, family leadership, godly character, and teaching and ministry skills.

Additionally, they are well aware of how their class or group fits into the larger purposes of the church. Adult Bible classes and groups have a unique opportunity to serve their church congregation as an entry point, an assimilation network, a shepherding outpost, and a ministry mobilization unit. As shepherds, leaders of these adult groups strive to provide a balance of biblical teaching, fellowship, healing, and equipping as they minister to and with their adult class.

Key #2—3-C Teachers

The most effective force an adult Bible ministry can have is a 3-C teacher, who follows the lead of the Holy Spirit. This teacher has compassion for others, knows the Bible well, and is willing to collaborate with the adult class members to facilitate optimum learning. The 3-C's of compassion, content, and collaboration are indispensable to the teacher of adults!

The effective teacher of adults also appreciates how God has made adult learners. He or she knows that adults are task-oriented, pragmatic, and intrinsically motivated. Adults appreciate learning from each other and from experience. They are unique individuals who think critically and like to be self-directed in their learning. Adult teachers respond to these qualities by becoming more of a guide than an expert. They become skilled facilitators of learning and use methods that are especially suited to adult learners. Since adults expect immediate applications, these teachers focus on how a passage applies to adults' personal and spiritual lives.

Key #3—Class Community

Every Christian needs to identify personally, on a first-name basis, with a group of other Christians with common needs and interests. This is fellowship. Believers can maintain casual relationships with many other Christians, but the mutual commitment level in these relationships may be low. It is an "I know you, I can identify with you, I am concerned about you, and I will pray for you" kind of commitment. Intimacy, however, is an interpersonal relationship that welcomes the baring of heart and soul. Effective adult Bible classes and groups seek to provide smaller, close care groups where spiritual intimacy can develop.

These adult groups know that learning and warm fellowship go hand in hand. As individuals feel accepted, comfortable, and cared for both during and outside the class times, they will participate more frequently and with greater confidence. And when class members are participating, they are learning. Therefore, the teaching sessions and group discussions will be more meaningful, and learning will be more effective for all the participants.

Key #4—Learning Environment

Whether they meet in a building or in a home, effective adult classes and groups seek to create an environment conducive to learning. They make sure there is enough space and flexibility for innovative learning activities, such as small group discussions, panel discussions, or role plays. They have taken care to choose room decorations that create a warm and inviting atmosphere. They have also paid attention to the more technical matters of light, sound, technology, and other instructional resources.

However, they also know that the physical environment of their class is not enough. The teacher and other class members can create a relaxed, informal atmosphere that allows everyone to learn in a positive, comfortable, and encouraging environment. Through eye contact, verbal affirmation, balanced participation, and a skillful and gentle guiding of learners into lesson goals, a gifted adult facilitator will create a genuine spirit of compassion and caring in the class.

Key #5—Individual Learning Needs

Effective adult education for one is effective adult education for all. This is why the best adult classes and groups focus on the individual needs of each adult participant and often involve these participants in forming class goals and selecting curriculum. An adult class may be made up of men and women, both married and single, from different cultural backgrounds and various generational segments. They will each have different learning needs, developmental needs, and personal needs. Several may be experiencing a physical disability, a learning disability, or other kind of disability. The wise adult teacher is sensitive to these individual needs, balancing them with larger group and community needs, as well as Scriptural goals.

A learning situation that teaches scriptural truth through collaboration, experiential learning, multiple methods, practical application, and a balanced focus on relationship and task will be the most conducive to meeting the needs of diverse learners.

Key #6—Learner Participation

Educational programs that lead to learning are interactive. Presenting content is not learning or, as one educator put it, "telling is not teaching." Adult Bible classes and groups that experience effective learning integrate activities throughout the session that allow participants to interact with the truths of the lesson. This often includes small group and large group discussions, projects, role plays, worksheets, and any form of getting class members involved in learning Biblical truth.

Teaching adults is a special experience because so much knowledge, wisdom, and expertise is represented among the group participants. Effective learning, therefore, is enhanced by the degree of collective insights with fellow group members. The effective teacher of adults does not feel that he or she has to provide all the answers or information. Rather, a teacher creates an open environment for learning in the group, inviting and encouraging all members to participate.

Key #7—Bible-focused Learning

The Bible is the textbook for every adult Bible class or group, regardless of the topic. Many churches focus the subject of their adult classes and groups on practical topics, such as marriage and family, practical Christian living, and stewardship. However, for the Christian, the Bible is the textbook of all of life. Even in topical studies, the Bible should still be the primary source of all that is taught. In essence, every adult Bible class or group in the church is just that, a Bible class. Even topical studies are, in essence, biblical studies.

In addition to topical biblical classes, a major need among churched adults today, however, is still Bible knowledge. This is not just isolated knowledge of specific Bible books or passages but an overall knowledge of Scripture. Churches that experience effective adult learning maintain their primary focus on the Bible. This not only includes exegetical verse-by-verse studies of isolated books, but Bible survey overviews as well. Adults must know how each section of the Bible relates to the other sections and to the Bible as a whole, and they must also know how to read and study the Bible on their own. A major focus, therefore, of every adult learning event is to help adults experience hands-on how to use all the Bible-related resources to understand God's Word more fully.

Summary

Adult Bible learning is crucial for today's church and today's Christian. Adults are the key to the cause of Christ both inside and outside the church. And God has given us the responsibility and the opportunity to guide the learning of His people so they are prepared to lead others and serve Him. How could any job be more exciting and fulfilling?

Our task, though, is to help adults learn. We do that by remembering the seven keys—vision for teaching, 3-C teachers, class community, learning environment, individual learning needs, learner participation, and Bible-focused learning. The result? Adults who know the Bible and know how to apply it to their lives to become active followers of Christ and leaders and ministers to others.

For Further Discussion

1. List all the opportunities available for adult learning. Compare this list to the suggestions provided under "Settings for Learning" in this chapter. What possible environments could be added to your church program?

2. Look again at the seven keys to effective learning. Which of these do you see as the most crucial key? Why?

3. What is the current learning status of your adult class? If learning is occurring, what factors are contributing to it? If learning is not occurring, analyze possible reasons. What keys are missing?

4. Meet with your church's leaders, leaders of other adult classes and groups, and perhaps adult class members as well, and map out a long-term strategy for creating effective adult learning for your church. Identify possible C-factored teachers and discuss how to integrate them into teaching opportunities.

Bibliography

Anderson, James A. "Cognitive Styles and Multicultural Populations." *Journal of Teacher Education* 39 (1988): 2–9.

Arn, Charles, Donald McGavran, and Win Arn. *Growth: A New Vision for the Sunday School.* Pasadena: Church Growth Press, 1980.

Barnard, Tom. *How to Grow an Adult Class.* Kansas City, Mo.: Beacon Hill Press, 1983.

Carroll, Colleen. *The New Faithful: Why Young Adults are Embracing Christian Orthodoxy.* Chicago: Loyola Press, 2002.

Edgerly, George A., and Harold E. Crosby. *Strategies for Sunday School Growth.* Springfield, Mo.: Gospel Publishing House, 1983.

Fawcett, Cheryl. *Understanding People.* Wheaton, Ill.: Evangelical Training Association, 2000.

Felder, Cain Hope. *Troubling Biblical Waters: Race, Class, and Family.* Mary Knoll, NY: Orbis Books, 1989.

Friere, Paulo. *Education for Critical Consciousness.* New York: Seabury Press, 1973.

Gallagher, David P. *Senior Adult Ministry in the 21st Century.* Loveland, Colo.: Group, 2002.

Galloway, Chester O. *Team Teaching With Adults.* Kansas City, Mo.: Beacon Hill Press, 1972.

Gangel, Kenneth O. *24 Ways to Improve Your Teaching.* Wheaton, Ill.: Victor, 1986.

Gangel, Kenneth O., and James C. Wilhoit. *The Christian Educator's Handbook on Adult Education.* Grand Rapids: Baker, 1993.

Gardner, Howard. *Multiple Ingelligences: The Theory in Practice.* New York: Basic Books, 1993.

Gilligan, Carol. *In a Different Voice.* Harvard: Harvard University Press, 1983.

Gorman, Julie. *Community That Is Christian: A Handbook on Small Groups.* Wheaton, Ill.: Victor Books, 1993.

Guy, Talmadge C., ed. *Providing Culturally Relevant Adult Education: A Challenge for the Twenty-first Century.* New Directions for Adult and Continuing Education, no. 82. San Francisco: Jossey-Bass, summer1999.

Hicks, Rick, and Kathy Hicks. *Boomers, Xers, and Other Strangers.* Wheaton, Ill.: Tyndale, 1999.

Howe, Neil, and William Strauss. *Millenials Rising: The Next Great Generation.* New York: Vintage Books, 2000.

Knowles, Malcom S. *The Modern Practice of Adult Education: From Pedagogy to Andragogy.* 2d ed. New York: Cambridge Books, 1980.

Larson, Knute. *Growing Adults on Sunday Morning.* Wheaton, Ill.: Victor Books, 1991.

LeFever, Marlene D. *Creative Teaching Methods.* Colorado Springs: David C. Cook, 1985, 1996.

_____. *Learning Styles: Reaching Everyone God Gave You to Teach.* Colorado Springs: David C. Cook, 1995.

Levinson, Daniel J. *The Seasons of a Man's Life*. New York: Ballatine Books, 1978.

Lindeman, Eduard C. *The Meaning of Adult Education*. New York: New Republic, 1926.

Marlowe, Monroe, and Bobbie Reed. *Creative Bible Learning for Adults*. Ventura, Calif.: Regal Books, 1977.

McCarthy, Bernice. *About Teaching: 4Mat in the Classroom*. Wauconda, Ill.: About Learning, Inc., 2000.

McCray, Walter Arthur. *The Black Presence in the Bible*. Chicago: Black Light Fellowship, 1990.

Merriam, Sharan B., and Rosemary S. Caffarella. *Learning in Adulthood*. 2d ed. San Francisco: Jossey-Bass, 1999.

Mezirow, Jack. *Learning as Transformation*. San Francisco: Jossey-Bass, Inc., 2000.

Murray, Dick. *Strengthening the Adult Sunday School Class*. Nashville: Abingdon Press, 1981.

Richards, Lawrence O., and Gary J. Bredfeldt. *Creative Bible Teaching*. Chicago: Moody Press, 1998.

Sell, Charles M. *Transitions Through Adult Life*. Grand Rapids: Zondervan, 1991.

Sheehy, Gail. *Passages: Predictable Crises of Adult Life*. New York: Bantam Books, 1974.

Shotwell, Larry. *Breakthrough: Adult Sunday School Work*. Nashville: Convention Press, 1990.

Thigpen, Jonathan N., ed. *Teaching Techniques*. Wheaton, Ill.: Evangelical Training Association, 2001.

Tough, Allen. *The Adult's Learning Projects: A Fresh Approach to Theory and Practice in Adult Learning*. Toronto: Ontario Institute for Studies in Education, 1971.

Towns, Elmer. *154 Steps to Revitalize Your Sunday School and Keep Your Church Growing*. Wheaton: Victor Books, 1988.

Wilbert, Warren N. *Teaching Christian Adults*. Grand Rapids: Baker Book House, 1980.

Wilkerson, Barbara, ed. *Multicultural Religious Education*. Birmingham, Ala.: Religious Education Press, 1997.

Paul, Richard, and Linda Elder. *The Miniature Guide to Critical Thinking Concepts & Tools*. N.p.: The Foundation for Critical Thinking, 2001.